Technology Projects

for Library Media Specialists and Teachers

Patricia Ross Conover

Linworth
Books

*Professional Development Resources for K-12
Library Media and Technology Specialists*

Published by Linworth Publishing, Inc.
480 East Wilson Bridge Road, Suite L
Worthington, OH 43085

Copyright © 2007 by Linworth Publishing, Inc.

Conover, Patricia Ross.
 Technology projects for library media specialists and teachers / Patricia Ross Conover.
    p. cm.
 ISBN 1-58683-223-9 (pbk.)
 1. Educational technology. 2. Middle school education--Computer-assisted instruction. 3. Middle school libraries--Activity programs. 4. Computers--Study and teaching (Middle school) 5. Information retrieval--Study and teaching (Middle school) 6. Research--Study and teaching (Middle school) I. Title.
 LB1028.3.C6626 2006
 371.33'4--dc22

                     2006026940

5 4 3 2 1

Table
of Contents

CHAPTER 3 - Research and show what you know 89

Conclusion 125

Table
of Figures

About
the Author

Pat Conover is a middle school library media specialist in Shawnee Mission, Kansas. She has been a librarian for eleven years, two in New Jersey, and nine in Kansas. Pat started her career in education as a second grade teacher, moved on to middle school math teacher and from there to library media specialist. Libraries, books, and middle school students have been the center of attention for many years. Add the extra component of technology, and it's all a perfect match.

Pat graduated from Cedar Crest College in Allentown, Pennsylvania with a B.A. in history and elementary education, from Montclair State University, Montclair, New Jersey, with an Educational Media Specialist's certificate, and a Master's Degree in Educational Technology from MidAmerica Nazarene University in Olathe, Kansas.

Acknowledgements

This book is dedicated to Barry for his ever-present encouragement, support, and faith in me, and to Bryn for her wonderful enthusiasm.

Introduction

What learning do you remember from your years in school? Do you remember the projects that you made? In second grade, our teacher helped us make pâpier-mâché fruits and vegetables to sell at a farm stand made out of a big cardboard box. I still remember both hoping that my classmates would buy the peaches that I had made and then making change when it was my time to be the salesperson. I know that the igloo I made out of sugar cubes fired in me an intense curiosity to know more about the Inuit, Aleut, and Yupik peoples and cultures. The shadow box Homer Price book report with the stacked and glued cheerio donuts on the diner counter was a fun and meaningful way for me to entice my classmates to read my favorite book. We all remember the things we make with own hands and creative thoughts. Students today enjoy using technology to seek information then prepare and present projects that demonstrate what they have learned. There are academic benefits for students from finding information, synthesizing it, and then producing hands-on projects, which creatively show teachers and their peers what they have learned.

Technology Projects for Library Media Specialists and Teachers provides library media specialists and classroom teachers with lesson plans and ideas for technology-based projects. The projects, which can be adapted to many grade levels and curricula, are created using Microsoft Word®, Microsoft PowerPoint®, and Microsoft Excel® programs. Clear, concise instructions are provided as well as correlations to American Library Association (ALA) Power Standards and National Educational Technology Standards (NETS).

With this in mind, read this book to discover ideas for projects, with comprehensive directions, for those times when you or a fellow teacher want to try something new, different, and exciting. Hands-on learning and project-based learning are effective with students of all ages. The projects generated by the students will challenge them not only to research information but also to demonstrate and communicate what they have learned in a meaningful fashion. Since a large portion of a library media specialist's job is to be a resource for teachers, take advantage of the student-tested lesson plans in this book.

The ideas and projects in this book come from a variety of sources and resources, from print and online to activities that fellow teachers or I have done with students. One of the greatest attributes of library media specialists and teachers is the ability to share ideas. More and more technology projects are posted on the Internet every day. Do a Web search for "technology projects for students," "technology arts and crafts," or "educational technology projects" and you will see incredible numbers of sites pertaining to educational technology. Many projects are those that have been created with the old "cut and paste" techniques. "Cut and paste" takes on a new dimension when using software programs. While the Web offers many cut and paste projects, my goal is to consolidate and provide a set of field-tested, standards-based, hands-on lessons that work as written. These projects are beyond cut and paste and are designed to lead students to use technology to communicate, in a powerful and meaningful way, what they have learned. The synthesis and evaluation levels in Bloom's Taxonomy will be attained. Students will use higher-order thinking skills as they experiment with new ideas and approaches. Please modify the projects in this book to make them work for you and your students.

The purpose of *Technology Projects for Library Media Specialists and Teachers* is to promote collaborative efforts between teachers, library media specialists, learning center teachers, English Language Learner teachers (ELL), support staff, and all who work with students. Because the main goal of our profession is to encourage every child to learn, we need to not only work together to make this happen but to also take full advantage of the technology resources available. By its very nature, technology provides tools for every child to succeed by adapting well to individual needs. I have seen students with disabilities create outstanding, imaginative projects because they were able to express their knowledge in a graphically friendly interface, such as PowerPoint. Technology stretches to encompass all students' needs, whether a physical, language, or motivational limitation. Students respond positively to using computer programs because they have grown up in a visually stimulating world.

The first section of the book is devoted to projects that are fun to create. You will be helping students craft lanterns, bag tags, banners, posters, candy bar wrappers, and more. The projects in the second section teach students to publish reports in different formats. Using PowerPoint to publish books, Word to create business cards, or Excel to produce banners and posters, you will teach students to display information in inventive ways. The third section is devoted to research-driven activities. While creating minibooks, post cards, table tents, culture cards, and more, students will demonstrate originality and expanded knowledge in special formats.

Directions have been written for Microsoft software of Word, PowerPoint, and Excel. Many of the projects can also be created using Microsoft's Publisher. However, Publisher is not as readily available to students as are Word, PowerPoint, and Excel. Teach students basic technology skills in Word, PowerPoint, and Excel and they can easily transfer what they have learned into Publisher or similar programs. This book provides detailed instructions for Microsoft software. When the software changes, the directions will still be usable. Just experiment a bit and look at the toolbars, icons, or help menu to find similar parts of updated programs.

Time is valuable to library media specialists and teachers. This book offers lesson plans, which correlate with the Information Literacy Standards for Student Learning from the American Library Association (ALA) and the National Educational Standards for Students (NETS) from the International Society for Technology in Education (ISTE). Teachers are experts at recognizing what students are capable of achieving, adapting lessons to students' abilities, and modifying the requirements accordingly.

The instruction is divided into three sections: plan, prepare, and present. Planning in Part I provides information about the grade levels, subject areas, software requirements, and standards addressed. Part II consists of preparation that you and your colleagues need to accomplish in order to be comfortable, confident, and organized before teaching the lesson. The presentation portion, Part III, is the work that takes place with your students. Part III is written succinctly and directly with clear, concise, and systematic directions to help you teach the lessons.

Evaluation of projects and student work is subjective. Each of us has a different style of grading based on the goals that the project has to meet and the learning standards that vary from state to state. The informational component is scored, as are the technology and presentation portions. As with any project, technology based or otherwise, students must have all of the information in their projects before the "bells and whistles" are added. With technology assignments, a rubric can assist in grading students' work. A great way to differentiate the lessons for gifted students is to assign the task of preparing a rubric for the project to these students. Self-evaluation is as important in most assignments as teacher and peer evaluations.

Many Web sites will create rubrics for you or give you ideas for how to prepare your own. Several are as follows:

❖ *http://rubistar.4teachers.org/index.php*

❖ *http://www.ncsu.edu/midlink/ho.html*

❖ *http://webquest.sdsu.edu/rubrics/weblessons.htm*

❖ *http://projects.edtech.sandi.net/staffdev/tpss99/rubrics/rubrics.html*

❖ *http://edtech.kennesaw.edu/intech/rubrics/htm*

I have included samples of two rubrics that I have used. The first is for the timelines project and the second for posters. A rubric can be prepared to measure anything that you think is important to the students' learning; it can identify and assess many requirements of the project or just a few. Your determination of the goals and standards to be met is key to a successful rubric. Discuss with your students what the requirements are for their projects as well as the importance of fulfilling all of these. In each of the rubrics shown, content accuracy and knowledge gained are the primary focus.

figure **0.1**

Timeline of...

Student name: _____

CATEGORY	4	3	2	1
Content/Facts	Facts were accurate for all events reported on the timeline.	Facts were accurate for almost all events reported on the timeline.	Facts were accurate for most (~75%) of the events reported on the timeline	Facts were often inaccurate for events reported on the timeline.
Learning of Content	The student can accurately describe 75% (or more) of the events on the timeline.	The student can accurately describe 50% of the events on the timeline.	The student can describe any event on the timeline if allowed to refer to it.	The student cannot use the timeline effectively to describe events nor to compare events.
Resources	The timeline contained at least 8-10 events related to the topic.	The timeline contained at least 6-7 events related to the topic.	The timeline contained at least 5 events related to the topic.	The timeline contained fewer than 5 events.
Preparation	The student had notes about all the events and dates to include on the timeline before beginning to design the timeline.	The student had notes about almost all the events and dates to include on the timeline before beginning to design the timeline.	The student had notes about most (~75%) of the events and dates to include on the timeline before beginning to design the timeline.	The student had not prepared adequate notes before beginning to design the timeline.
Time Use	Classroom time was used to work on the project.	Classroom time was used to work on the project the majority of the time.	Classroom time was poorly used to work on the project.	Student did not use classroom time to work on the project and/or was disruptive.
Graphics	All graphics are effective and balanced with text use.	All graphics are effective, but there appear to be too few or too many.	Some graphics are effective and their use is balanced with text use.	Several graphics are not effective.
Readability	The overall appearance of the timeline is pleasing and easy to read.	The overall appearance of the timeline is somewhat pleasing and easy to read.	The timeline is relatively readable.	The timeline is difficult to read.

figure 0.2

Wanted...

Student name: _____

CATEGORY	4	3	2	1
Content– Accuracy	At least 7 accurate facts are displayed on the poster.	5-6 accurate facts are displayed on the poster.	3-4 accurate facts are displayed on the poster.	Less than 3 accurate facts are displayed on the poster.
Knowledge Gained	Student can accurately answer all questions related to facts in the poster and processes used to create the poster.	Student can accurately answer most questions related to facts in the poster and processes used to create the poster.	Student can accurately answer about 75% of questions related to facts in the poster and processes used to create the poster.	Student appears to have insufficient knowledge about the facts or processes used in the poster.
Graphics– Relevance	All graphics are related to the topic and make it easier to understand. All borrowed graphics have a source citation.	All graphics are related to the topic and most make it easier to understand. All borrowed graphics have a source citation.	All graphics relate to the topic. Most borrowed graphics have a source citation.	Graphics do not relate to the topic OR several borrowed graphics do not have a source citation.
Attractiveness	The poster is exceptionally attractive in terms of design, layout, and neatness.	The poster is attractive in terms of design, layout, and neatness.	The poster is acceptably attractive though it may be a bit messy.	The poster is messy or carelessly designed.

If you are not yet entirely comfortable teaching technology skills to groups of 25-30 students and feel that you do not have enough eyes, ears, and hands to accomplish the lesson successfully, remember to utilize the expertise of your students. Enlist their help and value their knowledge. Students make excellent helpers, aids, and assistants. This approach not only takes the pressure off you but also allows students to be leaders in the classroom.

Students are adept at using technology. They are coming to us with highly developed skills and need to be motivated to put those skills to beneficial use. *Technology Projects for Library Media Specialists and Teachers* will help you to challenge your students and have fun yourself. What could be better?

Directions
for using this book

Technology Projects for School Media Specialists and Teachers is a resource for busy librarians and teachers. If you have never taught a technology-based lesson, be brave, pick one that appeals to you, and try it. This book will help you. Your students will enjoy the hands-on projects. If you have taught technology-based lessons for years, I hope that you will find several new and different ideas to enhance the program that you now have.

Lessons are written with **plan**, **prepare**, and **present** sections. Each lesson is introduced with a task description, suggestions as to how the projects can be used, and a photograph of the project. The picture of each project precedes the task description, which suggests ideas for curricular tie-ins. Please use your imagination and creativity to adapt the projects to your curriculum, standards, and age level of your students.

The **plan** section details curricular connections, grade levels, subject areas, Information Standards for Student Learning from ISTE, NETS Standards, and the software required. Most projects can easily fit into math, reading, language arts, and science curricula, which are the subject areas being stressed for national testing. However, consider using the lessons and project ideas for social studies, science, library, music, art, family and consumer science (FACS), industrial technology, international languages, health, physical education, other electives, and exploratory classes.

The second section, **prepare**, is a guideline for you, as you get ready to teach the lesson. It lists what you have to know and do prior to teaching your students. The detailed and systematic directions are in the **present** portion of the lesson. In this section, I have written the steps in exactly the same way that I teach my students. I have found that short, direct commands work best in technology lessons. Screen shots display what the computer screen should look like when creating the project because screen shots, diagrams, and illustrations help me when I attempt any new skill. In several of the lessons, I have listed suggested Web sites to help you. Know that I also still firmly believe in having print resources available for students to use.

In the third section, **present**, enlist the help of a colleague and team-teach. You will each have more fun, as will the students. Decide who will "drive" and who will "fly." The "driver" stands at the computer and models for students what steps to take. The "fly" flies around the room and helps students who are lost, on the wrong step, or otherwise not on task. Use a video projector, white board, or a TV monitor linked to the computer with an S-Cable to demonstrate the necessary techniques. If you can help it, do not face the daunting world of technology alone. A rule that I have always used with any technology enhanced project is that the students must have all of the information written in their projects before they add any of the fantastic extras. No changing font colors, sizes, graphics, or manipulating WordArt and background colors, until the content is in place. Be strict about this because, after all is said and done, the information presented and learned is the most important component of any project.

Technology assignments are well suited to collaborative learning. When students at various performance levels work together in small groups, success will be achieved. You know your students, how they work together, can judge what they are capable of accomplishing, and can group the students accordingly. Students with disabilities achieve success with technology projects because of the adaptive nature of the technology. Gifted students, English Language Learners (ELL), and special needs students all can benefit from the following:

❖ *Accommodate students learning styles.*

❖ *Adjust the pacing and variation of the end project.*

❖ *Allow for multiple intelligence options.*

❖ *Determine which students are strong in linguistic, logical mathematical, spatial, bodily kinesthetic, musical, interpersonal, intrapersonal, and naturalist intelligences.*

❖ *Have students tear illustrations from magazines, scan, and save them for use in projects.*

❖ *Create tiered lessons with the content being the same but the resulting projects being different.*

❖ *Provide a "Think-Pair-Share" grouping method. Students of all levels work and help each other.*

These projects and lessons can be accelerated for gifted and talented students as well as modified for ELL and special needs students. The differentiations table for gifted, ELL, and special needs students has ideas to try to address all students' abilities and learning styles.

For the highest level of success and the lowest level of stress with technology projects, please remember to:

❖ *Practice the skills needed in each lesson, found in the **present** section.*

❖ *Enlist the help of a colleague, or two. Do not face this challenge alone.*

❖ *Maintain a sense of humor. Things will go wrong.*

❖ *Have student helpers, lots of them. They will be as happy to help, as you will be to have their assistance.*

❖ *Read the directions, experiment with creating the project, and if you do not succeed, ask a student to work with you. Students will understand the instructions and help you.*

❖ *Experiment, be brave, save often, and have fun!*

figure **0.3**

Differentiation Table

Consider The Following Differentiation:		
Gifted	**ELL**	**Special Needs**
Adjust questions to advance the level of thinking of student response.	Divide instruction into shorter segments.	Seat close to the teacher, or to a student who is a helper.
Allow students to shift content area from facts, definitions, and descriptions to concepts, relationships, and generalizations.	Dedicate support staff or volunteer to work with ELL students.	Dedicate support staff or volunteer to work with special needs students.
Ask students to develop an assessment rubric for the assignment.	Create and laminate a copy of the written directions for the task. Include clip art illustrations to clarify.	Create and laminate a copy of the written directions for the task. Include clip art illustrations to clarify.
Ask students to pre-select a supply of clip art and copy it to a file for the class to share.	Make a sound recording of the directions so that students can repeatedly hear the directions.	Make a sound recording of the directions so that students can repeatedly hear the directions.
Assess student knowledge beforehand.	Introduce and develop new vocabulary visually.	Provide repetition of assignment; repeat, restate, rephrase, review, and reread.
Have students brainstorm and develop intuitive approaches.	Work one-on-one with students as time permits.	Work one-on-one with students as time permits.
Explore content area in greater depth.	Allow shortened assignments.	Allow shortened assignments.
Students present programs and projects to younger students.	Pair ELL students with strong speakers and writers.	Pair special needs students with strong speakers and writers.
Provide challenging work for those who can master basic skills.	Encourage and allow non-verbal responses such as pointing, nodding, pictures, and manipulatives.	Allow students to dictate reports and responses. Utilize recording technology.
Provide open-ended questions. These questions require higher-level thinking.	Extend assignments over a longer period.	Extend assignments over a longer period.
Student can choose a topic of interest and do independent study.	Encourage students to use native language for vocabulary.	Prepackage a file of images or clip art for students who need limited choices.
Students have choices of acquisition of information.	Allow for more use of images than text to explain subject matter.	Allow for more use of images than text to explain subject matter.
Students have content choices to select a parallel topic.	An aide works one on one with students.	An aide works one on one with students.
Students have product choices to demonstrate learning.	Create a file that is the "skeleton" of the assignment.	Create a file that is the "skeleton" of the assignment

Chapter One
Think outside the box
and have fun while doing it!

The projects presented in Chapter 1 are fun for you to teach and for students to create. These projects are tried and true, student and teacher tested, and are the activities that your students will remember long past the due date. Students will be perfecting their technology skills as well as displaying information learned. Many of the projects in Chapter 1 are ideally suited for bulletin board or tabletop displays. Add a banner or poster created in Excel and your bulletin board worries are over. Clear, concise, and illustrated directions are provided for each Word, Excel, or PowerPoint project. Practice the techniques and skills first and make a sample or two to show your students. In this way, you can estimate how long it will take your students to complete the project.

Lessons and project ideas can be adapted to the number of computers available. Whether you have access to one computer per class or one per student, these projects can still be made. The fewer computers available, the more scheduling work and grouping considerations you will have. Talk with your colleagues to see how they have arranged these scheduling issues. Do you have access to laptops? If so, schedule them for your students to use.

When tackling technology lessons, the best advice I can give you is to maintain your sense of humor. *When,* not *if,* things do not go as planned, try to be as flexible as you can possibly be. The next best piece of advice I have is to enlist the help of your students. You will be surprised which students become the best and brightest technology stars. Let them shine! The help they can give you will make the difference between all of you enjoying the technology portion of your class or not. If you teach young children, ask older ones if they can help. The collaborative possibilities are numerous.

While you are reading Chapter 1, be thinking of ways you will adapt the technology projects to your students and curriculum. Take time to *think outside the box and have fun!* Your class will be an exciting place when students are working diligently on creative, hands-on, and fun projects.

figure **1.1**

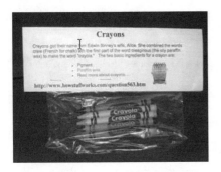

Information Literacy Standards for Student Learning

The student who is information literate uses information accurately and creatively.

The student who is an independent learner is information literate and pursues information related to personal interests.

NETS Standards:

Students are proficient in the use of technology.

Students use technology tools to enhance learning, increase productivity, and promote creativity.

BAG TAGS
Great for displays!

Task Description: Students will create a label to attach to a sandwich sized zip lock bag. Anything can be in this bag with information about the contents listed on the bag tag. Bag tags are a terrific way to display and identify small items.

I. PLAN

Curricular Connections:

Display of items for "how stuff works." For example, what does a bobbin do in a sewing machine?

Display of things that students collect.

Number of items for younger students, as in three pencils, six crayons.

Science—rocks, minerals, leaves, plants, and seeds.

Ingredients for recipes.

Items from sewing class or woodshop.

Grade levels: All

Subject Areas:

Elective Areas

Language Arts

Library

Mathematics

Science

Social Studies

Software: Word

II. PREPARE

❑ *Decide topics to be displayed.*

❑ *Prepare a schedule for each student, if necessary, based on number of computers available.*

❑ *Practice changing margins in Word.*

❑ *Practice using the ruler in Word.*

❑ *Practice how to create bag tag and assemble project.*

❑ *Practice inserting text boxes, ClipArt, and WordArt.*

III. PRESENT

Step 1: Discuss how bag tag works. Careful editing is essential in order to fit the information into small spaces. Display examples of tagged items and encourage students to get creative with the contents and labeling of the bag.

Step 2: Demonstrate skills needed by students in Word.

Step 3: Open **Word**. Go to **File, New.** Select **Blank document**.

Step 4: Go to **File**, **Page Setup**. Change **Margins** to:
Top 0 inches
Bottom 0 inches
Left 0.5 inches
Right 0.5 inches

Step 5: Pop-up will appear. Click **Ignore**.

Step 6: Go to **View**, click on **Ruler**. Seeing and using the ruler along the sides of the screen enables correct text position.

Step 7: Go to **Insert**, **Text Box**. Type title and facts about contents of the bag in the area between 5 1/2 inches and 8 1/4 inches. As shown, fold the paper into four parts. The information is entered in the third section of the page.

Step 8: Go to **Insert**, **Picture**, **ClipArt**. Choose appropriate images.

Step 9: Go to **Insert**, **Picture**, **WordArt** to add interesting WordArt to project.

Step 10: Go to **File**, **Print** on 8 1/2 x 11-inch paper.

Step 11: Fold the paper in half. Open and fold both ends into the centerfold. Staple to the zip lock bag.

figure **1.2**

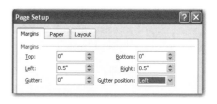

figure **1.3**

figure **1.4**

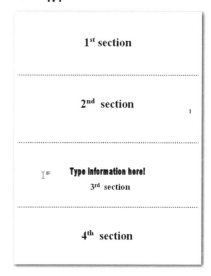

figure **1.5**

Information Literacy Standards for Student Learning

The student who is information literate uses information accurately and creatively.

The student who is information literate accesses information efficiently and effectively.

NETS Standards:

Students demonstrate a sound understanding of the nature and operation of technology systems.

Students are proficient in the use of technology.

Students use technology tools to enhance learning, increase productivity, and promote creativity.

BANNERS
Create colorful bulletin boards and displays!

Task Description: Students work in Excel to produce banners for bulletin boards or displays. Making banners is an excellent use of Excel and demonstrates that Excel can be used for creative purposes as well as spreadsheets. This project is fun for students and practical for teachers. Making banners not only saves you money and trips to the teacher supply store but also allows you and your students to customize displays and advertisements.

I. PLAN

Curricular Connections:

Create posters for library displays and bulletin boards.

Celebrate new books that have arrived or a visiting author.

Announce upcoming events in the library and school.

Student projects.

Student activities bulletin boards.

For any reason at all, banners are always fun!

Grade levels: 3-12

Subject Areas: All

Software: Excel

II. PREPARE

❑ *Decide topics that need to be advertised with a banner.*

❑ *Prepare a schedule for each student, if necessary, based on number of computers available.*

❑ *Practice using Excel.*

❑ *Practice changing margins.*

❑ *Learn about the zoom feature in the view menu.*

❑ *Experiment with setting the print area.*

III. PRESENT

Step 1: Display a banner that you or students have created. Encourage creativity and imagination in using Excel.

Step 2: Demonstrate using the various parts of Excel.

Step 3: Open **Excel**, **New** document, **File**, **Page Setup**, change layout to **Landscape**.

Step 4: Go to **File**, **Page Setup**, **Margins** tab and change the **Margins** to:
Top .5 inches
Bottom .5 inches
Left .5 inches
Right .5 inches
Header and Footer 0 inches
Change **Layout** to **Landscape**.
Click **OK** to save changes.

Step 5: Go to **View**, **Zoom**. Select **Custom** view and change it to **40%**.
Click **OK**.
There will be multiple pages on the screen at one time. Dotted lines indicate natural page breaks.

Step 6: Highlight the number of pages needed for the banner. Four or five pages make a banner that is approximately 40 to 50 inches in length. Go to **File**, **Print Area**, and then **Set Print Area**. A heavier dotted line will outline the parameters of the banner.

Step 7: **Insert** pictures, shapes, textboxes, WordArt to create banner.

Step 8: Go to **File**, **Print**. Trim the .5-inch margins from the pages and paste or tape together. Laminate the banner for durability.

figure **1.6**

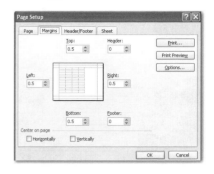

figure **1.7**

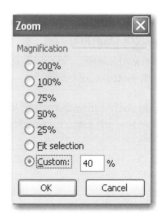

figure **1.8**

figure **1.9**

Information Literacy Standards for Student Learning

The student who is information literate accesses information efficiently and effectively.

The student who is information literate uses information accurately and creatively.

NETS Standards:

Students demonstrate a sound understanding of the nature and operation of technology systems.

Students are proficient in the use of technology.

BUILDING BLOCKS
See what you and your students can construct!

Task Description: Students will draw a block pattern in PowerPoint and insert text, graphics, and any other required information. Use the ruler, drawing toolbar, and all of the graphic bells and whistles available in PowerPoint to create these. This project takes a bit of patience but it is definitely worth the effort. If you need larger blocks and have a copy machine available, enlarge the 8 1/2 x 11-inch paper to 11 x 17-inch, which is a 140% enlargement.

I. PLAN

Curricular Connections:

Favorite books or characters on each of the six surfaces. Build a class wall!

Book report, fiction, or nonfiction.

Current events article with who, what, when, where, why, and how of the story.

Alphabet blocks, helpful to young students and ELL students.

Riddles - five clues with answer on the bottom of the block.

Following a written or verbal directions exercise.

Grade levels: 3-12

Subject Areas: All

Software: PowerPoint

II. PREPARE

❑ *Decide topics for the project.*

❑ *Prepare a schedule for each student, if necessary, based on number of computers available.*

❑ *Practice using the ruler in PowerPoint.*

❑ *Practice using the rectangle icon to draw perfect squares.*

❑ *Practice inserting text boxes, graphics, images, and WordArt.*

III. PRESENT

Step 1: Discuss the building block project. Provide samples of building blocks in various shapes that you or former students have made. Information needs to be carefully edited to fit in small spaces.

Step 2: Demonstrate PowerPoint skills needed by students.

Step 3: Open **PowerPoint**. Go to **File**, **New**. Select **Blank slide**.

Step 4: Go to **View**, select **Ruler**.

Step 5: **View**, **Toolbars**, select **Drawing**.

Step 6: Click on the **Rectangle** icon on the drawing toolbar, or **down arrow** at **AutoShapes** and select **Basic Shapes**.

Step 7: Using the ruler as a guide, select the **Rectangle** icon, hold down the **Ctrl** key, and draw a **2 1/4 x 2 1/4-inch** square. Right click on the square, **Copy**. Right click, **Paste**. Create **six** identical squares.

Step 8: Again using the ruler, click on the **Rectangle** icon and draw a **2 1/4-x 1/2-inch** rectangle. Do the same **Copy** and **Paste** technique making five identical rectangles, as seen in figure 1.12.

Step 9: Go to **Insert**, **Text Box**. Add information on each square of the block. Add images and WordArt. Get creative!

Step 10: Go to **File**, **Print**. Print on cardstock for more durability.

Step 11: Cut on solid lines, crease dotted lines, glue flaps to make the block.

figure **1.10**

figure **1.11**

figure **1.12**

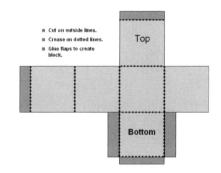

figure **1.13**

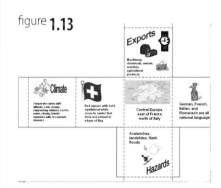

figure **1.14**

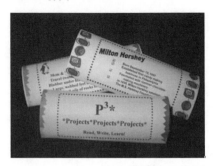

CANDY BAR WRAPPERS
Everyone loves a good candy bar!

Task Description: Students will research a topic and create a wrapper for a candy bar. This project makes a "sweet" bulletin board. Students get the fun of eating the chocolate bar as an added bonus. For display purposes, substitute pieces of cardboard cut to candy bar size and wrapped in foil. Be sure to experiment with the margins for the candy bars you are wrapping. Sizes tend to change frequently.

I. PLAN

Curricular Connections:

Quick project in the library, explaining how to use online databases or online catalog.

Poetry, haiku, limericks, or any other type of creative writing.

Inventors—who did what, when, where, and how.

Biography reports—the most important parts of that person's life.

Newspaper articles in the abridged edition.

Grade levels: All

Subject Areas:

Elective Areas

Language Arts

Library

Mathematics

Science

Social Studies

Software: Word

II. PREPARE

❑ *Decide topics to be researched.*

❑ *Prepare a schedule for each student, if necessary, based on number of computers available.*

❑ *Practice setting margins in Word.*

❑ *Practice finding and using ruler in Word.*

❑ *Practice using text boxes, inserting graphics and WordArt.*

Information Literacy Standards for Student Learning

The student who is information literate accesses information efficiently and effectively.

The student who is information literate evaluates information critically and competently.

The student who is information literate uses information accurately and creatively.

NETS Standards:

Students use technology tools to enhance learning, increase productivity, and promote creativity.

Students use technology tools to process data and report results.

III. PRESENT

Step 1: Discuss and introduce Candy Bar Wrapper project. Show samples and encourage creativity in students.

Step 2: Demonstrate how to change margins, use ClipArt, WordArt.

Step 3: In **Word**, open **New** document. Go to **File**, **Page Setup**. Change **Margins** to:
Top 1 inch
Bottom 4.5 inches
Left 1 inch
Right 1.5 inches

Step 4: Go to **Insert**, **Picture**, **ClipArt**. Search for **Page Border**. Select **Insert**. Pull on one of the four handles (corners) of ClipArt to fill the space. Watch the margins on the page.

Step 5: Go to **Insert**, **Text Box**, **4 inches wide**, and **2 inches long** within the border. Enter the design, words, poem, logo, or WordArt. Change fonts, colors, sizes, and alignment. Make sure to move, resize, and center the text box within the rectangle.

Step 6: **View**, **Toolbars**, select **Drawing**. Select Dash Style icon and Line Style icon to change size and style of text box.

Step 7: **File**, **Print**, and cut out the rectangle & wrap the candy bar. Tape edges.

figure **1.15**

figure **1.16**

figure **1.17**

figure **1.18**   figure **1.19**

figure **1.20**

Information Literacy Standards for Student Learning

The student who is information literate evaluates information critically and competently.

The student who is information literate uses information accurately and creatively.

NETS Standards:

Students are proficient in the use of technology.

Students use technology tools to enhance learning, increase productivity, and promote creativity.

CHECK IT OUT
Look no further for a way to recommend books!

Task Description: Students will write book reviews within a large check mark. This PowerPoint project is quick, easy, and enjoyable. The book reviews can be posted in the library, classroom, or on a bulletin board.

I. PLAN

Curricular Connections:

Display new books.

Book reviews done by students or faculty advertising and recommending favorite books.

Any information that needs attention drawn to it.

Grade levels: All

Subject Areas: All

Software: PowerPoint

II. PREPARE

❑ *Decide what will be "checked out."*

❑ *Prepare a schedule for each student, if necessary, based on number of computers available.*

❑ *Practice using PowerPoint, importing ClipArt checkmark.*

❑ *Practice inserting text box and text.*

❑ *Experiment with removing the line around the text box.*

III. PRESENT

Step 1: Discuss the concept of "checking things out." Determine which topics or books are to be assigned to students. Display samples.

Step 2: Demonstrate how to find a check mark in ClipArt, how to add the text box and then remove the line around it.

Step 3: Open **PowerPoint**. Choose **New, Blank Slide**.

Step 4: Go to **Insert, Picture, ClipArt**. Search for a checkmark and **Insert** that graphic. Pull on one of the four handles (corners) of the ClipArt to stretch it in proportion.

Step 5: Go to **Insert, Text Box**. Add the information needed.

Step 6: **Insert WordArt** and images too. Get inspired.

Step 7: Go to **View, Toolbars**, select **Drawing**. Drawing toolbar will appear on the bottom of the screen.

Step 8: **Right click** on the outside of the text box. Go to the **Line Color** icon (paintbrush) on the Drawing toolbar. **Down arrow** and select **No Line**. Fill entire slide with graphics and text.

Step 9: Go to **File, Print**. Cut out check mark and mount on colored paper for display purposes.

figure **1.21**

figure **1.22**

figure **1.23**

figure **1.24**

Strawberries
I love strawberries
All year round
They taste so delicious
But they don't make a sound!

Information Literacy Standards for Student Learning

The student who is an independent learner is information literate and pursues information related to personal interests.

The student who is information literate uses information accurately and creatively.

NETS Standards:

Students are proficient in the use of technology.

Students use productivity tools to collaborate in constructing technology-enhanced models, prepare publications, and produce other creative works.

FREEFORM PROSE
Add the visual element to student writings!

Task Description: Students will write their poetry within a shape that exemplifies the poem's meaning. Freeform prose allows students to be creative and to use PowerPoint as a publishing tool while encouraging originality and higher-level thinking. The results are awesome, inventive, and imaginative.

I. PLAN

Curricular Connections:

Poetry, haiku, limericks.

Creative writing projects.

Biography reports.

Holiday celebrations and explanations.

Country or state study.

Explanation of different cultures.

Grade levels: 2-8

Subject Areas: All

Software: PowerPoint

II. PREPARE

- ❏ *Decide topics for students' work.*
- ❏ *Prepare a schedule for each student, if necessary, based on number of computers available.*
- ❏ *Practice PowerPoint skills with graphics, drawing tools, and text boxes.*
- ❏ *Experiment with taking the outside line off the text box.*
- ❏ *Practice changing background colors and effects.*

III. PRESENT

Step 1: Discuss and introduce idea of freeform prose. Display examples.

Step 2: Demonstrate PowerPoint, importing graphics, working with freeform drawing tool, inserting text box.

Step 3: In **PowerPoint**, open **New Presentation, Blank Slide**.

Step 4: Go to **Insert, Picture, ClipArt**. Resize the graphic to fit the entire slide. Pull on one of four handles (corners) of image to resize to fit entire slide.

Step 5: Go to **View, Toolbars** and select **Drawing** Toolbar option. The Drawing toolbar appears at the bottom of the window. Down arrow **Auto Shapes, Lines, Freeform**.

Step 6: Click on **Freeform**. On the ClipArt image, a small pencil will appear as you draw around the outline. Freeform drawing takes patience and practice. Double click when the outline is finished to close the figure.

Step 7: "**Grab**" the original ClipArt and move it off the outline shape. **Delete ClipArt**, not drawing.

Step 8: On Drawing Toolbar, select icon for **Fill Color** (Paint Can), **down arrow** and select **No Fill**.

Step 9: Go to **Insert, Text Box**. Add poem to the text box.

Step 10: Go to **View, Toolbars**, select **Drawing**. Drawing toolbar will be at the bottom of the window. **Right click** on the outside of the text box. Go to the Line Color icon (paintbrush) on the Drawing toolbar. **Down arrow** and select **No Line**.

Step 11: **Right click** on slide background and select **Background. Down Arrow** to **Fill Effects**.

Step 12: Experiment with options in fill effects. Change Gradient, Texture, Pattern, Picture. This is the same technique used to change the backgrounds of images and text boxes.

Step 13: **File, Print**. Display.

figure **1.25**

figure **1.26**

figure **1.27**

figure **1.28**

figure **1.29**

figure **1.30**

figure **1.31**

figure **1.32**

Information Literacy Standards for Student Learning

The student who is an independent learner is information literate and appreciates literature and other creative expressions of information.

The student who is information literate uses information accurately and creatively.

NETS Standards:

Students are proficient in the use of technology.

Students use technology tools to enhance learning, increase productivity, and promote creativity.

IDIOMS ANYONE?
Have fun with the complexities of the English language!

Task Description: Students will create idiom word puzzles using ClipArt images to represent the words and connectors to join them. Idioms are confusing because the meaning of the group of words together has little, often nothing, to do with meanings of the words alone. Have students share their idiom puzzles with others. Guessing what the idiom puzzles mean is a very good way to begin a class and get everyone thinking. Students have fun with this project and enjoy challenging their peers and you.

I. PLAN

Curricular Connections:

Encourages higher level thinking skills.

Word games and puzzles.

Use word puzzles as introduction to class.

Grade levels: All

Subject Areas:

Language Arts - study of languages.

Library

Software: PowerPoint

II. PREPARE

❏ *Research idioms and compile a list for students or compile a list of Web sites. A quick search on Google.com will show many Web sites about idioms including http://www.idiomsite.com/, http://idioms. thefreedictionary.com/, or http://www.goenglish.com.*

❏ *Prepare a schedule for each student, if necessary, based on number of computers available.*

❏ *Practice using PowerPoint program graphics. Skills needed include importing graphics, resizing graphics, adding plus signs, equal signs.*

❏ *Prepare several samples of idiom images. Suggestions:*

Don't look a gift horse in the mouth.

Under the weather.

Rat race.

III. PRESENT

Step 1: Discuss idioms. Have several examples that you have prepared and have a handout of idioms or have books of idioms ready for students to use.

Step 2: Demonstrate how to work with graphics in PowerPoint, how to use AutoShapes on Drawing Toolbar.

Step 3: Open **PowerPoint**, **New**, choose **Blank Presentation**, then **Blank Slide**.

Step 4: Go to **Insert**, **Picture**, **ClipArt**. Select images that demonstrate the meaning of the words in the idiom.

Step 5: Go to **View**, **Toolbars**, select **Drawing**. Look for **AutoShapes**. **Down arrow** and experiment with **Connectors**, **Block Arrows**, and **Basic Shapes** that can be added to connect the images.

Step 6: Experiment to get the correct arrows and elbows! Select (click on) arrow. With that selected, **Down Arrow** and change the **Fill Color** (paintbrush) icon, **Line Style** (thin to thick line) icon, **Dash Style** (dotted lines icon), **Arrow Style** (arrow in different directions) icon, **Shadow Style** (Single green square) icon or **3-D Style** (green square with dimensions) icon.

Step 7: Go to **File**, **Print**, and have more fun than a barrel full of monkeys.

figure **1.33**

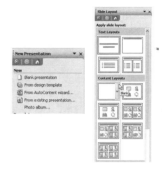

figure **1.34**

figure **1.35**

figure **1.36**

figure **1.37**

Information Literacy Standards for Student Learning

The student who is information literate uses information accurately and creatively.

The student who is an independent learner is information literate and appreciates literature and other creative expressions.

NETS Standards:

Students are proficient in the use of technology.

Students demonstrate a sound understanding of the nature and operation of technology systems.

Students use technology tools to enhance learning, increase productivity, and promote creativity.

LIGHT THE LANTERNS
Clever, creative, and a great hands-on project!

Task Description: Students will construct paper lanterns using PowerPoint. Authentic Chinese lanterns are traditionally giant red balls, but many are made in different shapes and colors. Lanterns add color and brightness to displays and can be hung from the ceiling for a beautiful effect.

I. PLAN

Curricular Connections:

Display item for study of Chinese New Year.

Study of Chinese art and culture.

Decorations for the classroom or library.

Grade levels: 3-12

Subject Areas:

Art

International Studies

Language Arts

Library

Social Studies

Software - PowerPoint

II. PREPARE

❑ *Decide what information lanterns will highlight.*

❑ *Prepare a schedule for each student, if necessary, based on number of computers available.*

❑ *Practice creating shapes in PowerPoint using Drawing Toolbar.*

❑ *Practice importing and working with ClipArt graphics.*

❑ *Experiment with changing font colors, background colors.*

III. PRESENT

Step 1: Introduce the history of Chinese lanterns. Show samples.

Step 2: Demonstrate skills and techniques needed in this project.

Step 3: Open **PowerPoint**, **New**, **Blank Presentation**. Select **Blank Slide**.

Step 4: Go to **View**, select **Ruler**.

Step 5: Go to **View**, **Toolbar**, and **Drawing**. The Drawing toolbar will appear on the lower left side of the program window.

Step 6: Click on the **Rectangle** icon. Using the ruler as a guide, draw the handle **1 1/2 x 10 inches**.

Step 7: **Down arrow** on **AutoShapes**. Select **Basic Shapes**. Select shape. Draw a shape **2 1/2 x 4 1/2 inches**. Right click on the shape, select **Copy**. Right click, select **Paste**. Create **three** additional shapes and space them side-by-side, leaving a small margin in between each shape and **1/2 inch** on left and right margins.

Step 8: Go to **Insert**, **Text Box**. Add text, graphics, WordArt to four shapes and handle.

Step 9: Group text boxes together so that the lantern, text, and graphics are all selected. Hold down the **Shift** key, and click on each shape, graphic, and text box. **Down arrow** at **Draw**, select **Group**.

Step 10: Click on lantern, select **Fill** icon (paint can) on **Drawing** toolbar. Change Gradient, Texture, Pattern, or Picture of background. Get as creative and artistic as possible.

Step 11: Go to **File**, **Print**. Cut out lantern along solid lines. Fold. Glue sides together. Cut out and attach handle.

figure **1.38**

figure **1.39**

figure **1.40**

figure **1.41**

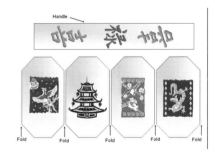

figure **1.42**

figure **1.43**

Jacobus Elementary Library
Phone: 800.256.3568
Library time is every Monday
8:30 to 9:20 am

Librarian: Mrs. Smith
Aide: Mrs. Jones

- 3 books each week!
- Return and get new!
- Lesson, story time, and book checkout!

Information Literacy Standards for Student Learning

The student who is information literate accesses information efficiently and effectively.

The student who is information literate uses information accurately and creatively.

NETS Standards:

Students are proficient in the use of technology.

Students demonstrate a sound understanding of the nature and operation of technology systems.

Students use technology tools to enhance learning, increase productivity, and promote creativity.

MAGNET MEMO
What an excellent advertisement for refrigerators and lockers!

Task Description: Using Avery® Magnet Sheets (#3270) or Avery® Magnetic Business Cards (#8374), students will create fun and fact filled magnets for lockers or home. Magnets also adhere to white boards in classrooms for an updated version of the flannel board. This is an excellent way to create magnetized messages, reminders, advertisements, and storyboard pieces.

I. PLAN

Curricular Connections:

Library information, such as day of the week or number of books allowed, for students.

Information of any kind to be posted at home or in lockers.

Storyboard images for white boards, similar to flannel board images.

Vocabulary lists to be displayed on white board.

Sequencing of ideas.

Grade levels: All

Subject Areas: All

Software: Word

II. PREPARE

❏ *Select topics to be "magnetized." Decide if students are creating one magnet out of the 10 per page, a freeform project on an entire sheet of magnetized paper, or attaching a magnetic strip to the back of a project printed on regular paper.*

❏ *Prepare a schedule for each student, if necessary, based on number of computers available.*

❏ *Practice using the label feature in Word.*

❏ *Practice inserting text and ClipArt.*

III. PRESENT

Step 1: Discuss and introduce making magnets to students. Show samples of your work or other students' work.

Step 2: Demonstrate how to use Word with the label tool. Demonstrate inserting text boxes, graphics, WordArt in Word.

Step 3: In **Word**, open **New**, select **Blank document**.

Step 4: Go to **Tools**, **Letters and Mailings**, **Envelopes and Labels**. Choose **Labels** tab (figure 2), and then **Options**. Select the **Product number**. (#8371 for business card size, #3270 for whole sheet of magnetized paper, or number that corresponds to the product). Click **OK**.

Step 5: Click on **New Document**.

Step 6: Go to **Table**, select **Show Gridlines**. Seeing the gridlines enables you to see the space allotted to each label and adjust text and graphics accordingly.

Step 7: Go to **Insert**, **Text Box** and type information into each label area.

Step 8: Go to **Insert**, **Picture**, **ClipArt** to add images and WordArt. Change fonts, colors, and sizes. This is fun!

Step 9: Check directions for printer. The settings may need adjustment to print magnet labels.

Step 10: **File**, **Print**, and distribute.

figure **1.44**

figure **1.45**

figure **1.46**

figure **1.47**

figure **1.48**

A. **Class-Aves** (includes all birds)
   ◦Have an outer covering of feathers
   ◦Endothermic (warm-blooded)
   ◦Front limbs modified as wings
   ◦Lay eggs
B. **Order-Sphenisciformes**
   ◦All living and extinct penguins.
C. **Family-Spheniscidae**
   ◦Includes all penguins, living and extinct
   ◦Only family classification in the order Sphenisciformes
D. **Genus, species**
   ◦Most scientists recognize 17 species of penguins

figure **1.49**

Information Literacy Standards for Student Learning

The student who is information literate uses information accurately and creatively.

The student who is an independent learner is information literate and strives for excellence in information seeking and knowledge generation.

NETS Standards:

Students are proficient in the use of technology.

Students use productivity tools to enhance learning, increase productivity, and promote creativity.

MINI BOOKS
This project is a guaranteed hit with students of all ages!

Task Description: Students will prepare slides in PowerPoint and print as handouts six per page. When cut apart and stapled together, a mini book is the product. Figure 1.48 is the entire mini book and figure 1.49 illustrates how the slides print as handouts six per page.

I. PLAN

Curricular Connections:

State or country reports

Book reports

Informational science or social studies reports

Any topic can be studied, researched, and made into a compact mini book.

Grade levels: 3-8

Subject Areas: All

Software: PowerPoint

II. PREPARE

❑ *Decide topics to be researched and studied.*

❑ *Prepare a schedule for each student, if necessary, based on number of computers available.*

❑ *Practice using PowerPoint.*

❑ *Be comfortable inserting graphics or images, text boxes.*

❑ *Review the options in the Print Dialog box. Look for* **Print What** *option, select* **Handouts**. *The default is six per page, which is required for this project.* **Frame Slides** *is the default, which is also good for this project.*

III. PRESENT

Step 1: Discuss mini book project and topics. Display examples.

Step 2: Demonstrate techniques of PowerPoint used to create this project. Demonstrate the print options and stress the importance of printing as handouts/six per page. If this option is not chosen, full size slides will print wasting paper and ink.

Step 3: Open **PowerPoint**, **New**, **Blank Presentation**. Select **Blank Slide**.

Step 4: Go to **Format**, **Slide Layout**. Choose slides that fit purpose, whether a **Title Only** slide, **Title and Text**, or even **Title and Table**.

Step 5: Insert information. Each slide is a finished page of the mini book. Text and graphics must fill the entire slide.

Step 6: Go to **Print**, **Print What**, **Handouts**, **6 per page**, and select **Frame Slides**. Click **OK**.

Step 7: Cut the handouts apart, adding a 1/2-inch margin to the left side of each page, and fasten books together.

figure **1.50**

figure **1.51**

figure **1.52**

Information Literacy Standards for Student Learning

The student who is information literate uses information accurately and creatively.

The student who is information literate accesses information efficiently and effectively.

NETS Standards:

Students demonstrate a sound understanding of the nature and operation of technology systems.

Students are proficient in the use of technology.

Students use technology tools to enhance learning, increase productivity, and promote creativity.

POSTERS
Excel can do more than create spreadsheets!

Task Description: Students will work in Excel to create posters. They import images, digital photographs, and use ClipArt or WordArt to produce this ingenious project. Posters are excellent additions to presentations and bulletin boards.

I. PLAN

Curricular Connections:

Each student creates a "Read" poster, importing digital image and highlighting a favorite book.

Any project that would benefit from a poster for explanatory or display purposes.

Grade levels: All

Subject Areas: All

Software: Excel, digital camera

II. PREPARE

❑ *Decide topics for posters.*

❑ *Go to ALA Web site to check out the READ software.*
http://www.alastore.ala.org/

❑ *Prepare a schedule for each student, if necessary, based on number of computers available.*

❑ *Practice using Excel, digital pictures, Microsoft Photo Editor.*

❑ *Take digital photographs of students.*

❑ *Practice how to adjust margins and view of Excel document.*

III. PRESENT

Step 1: Introduce, discuss, and display posters.

Step 2: Demonstrate in Excel the techniques of changing page setup, inserting pictures, WordArt.

Step 3: Open **Excel**, **New document**, **Blank Workbook**.

Step 4: Go to **File**, **Page Setup**, select the **Margins** tab, and change the **Margins** to:
Top .5 inches
Bottom .5 inches
Left .5 inches
Right .5 inches
Header and Footer 0 inches
Click **OK** to save changes.

Step 5: Go to **View**, **Zoom**. Select **Custom** view, change it to **40%**. Click **OK**.

Step 6: There will be multiple pages on the screen at one time. Dotted lines indicate natural page breaks. **Highlight four pages**, two on the top and two on the bottom.

Step 7: Go to **File**, **Print Area**, and **Set Print Area**. A heavier dotted line will now outline the parameters of the poster.

Step 8: **Insert** pictures, shapes, textboxes, WordArt to create a great poster. Have students save their own pictures to their picture file. Go to **Insert**, **Picture**, **From File**. Select the picture and resize or rotate using one of the "handles" (corners). To move the picture, place mouse over the picture or object. When the moving tool (two double pointed arrows in the shape of an X) displays, click and drag to the desired location. To rotate image, click on the green circle, which will enable you to swing that image around!

Step 9: Add background colors by selecting the four pages and using the Fill effects option on the drawing toolbar.

Step 10: Go to **File**, **Print**. Dotted lines will not print because they are just marking page breaks. Trim the **1/2-inch** margins from the pages and paste or tape together.

figure **1.53**

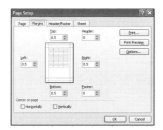

figure **1.54**

figure **1.55**   figure **1.56**

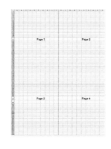

figure **1.57**

figure **1.58**

figure **1.59**

Information Literacy Standards for Student Learning

The student who is information literate uses information accurately and creatively.

The student who is information literate accesses information efficiently and effectively.

NETS Standards:

Students are proficient in the use of technology.

Students use technology tools to enhance learning, increase productivity, and promote creativity.

SHAPE BOOKS
Students publish their work within any selected shape!

Task Description: Students will write text within the outline of a shape. The cover, all of the pages, and the back cover are all made of the same shape. Students can add as many pages as needed. This project appeals to the younger students or to older students creating books for a younger audience. Working with the shape encourages creativity, imagination, good research, and story telling fun. This is a great creative writing project, which is fun for both the writer and the reader.

I. PLAN

Curricular Connections:

Favorite food report written in the shape of a pizza, burger, or fries.

Inventors and inventions - write about inventor in the shape of his invention.

Poetry, haiku, creative writing passages.

Science research about animals, vegetables, or minerals.

Grade levels: K-6

Subject Areas: All

Software: PowerPoint

II. PREPARE

❑ *Decide topics to be studied.*

❑ *Prepare a schedule for each student, if necessary, based on number of computers available.*

❑ *Practice accessing and inserting ClipArt in PowerPoint.*

❑ *Practice inserting textboxes, using them, and then deleting the line around the box.*

❑ *Experiment with fill effects for background*

III. PRESENT

Step 1: Introduce topic to students. Show examples of shape books.

Step 2: Review PowerPoint and all features required for this assignment.

Step 3: Open **PowerPoint**, **File**, **New**, **Blank Presentation**. Select **Blank Slide**.

Step 4: Go to **Insert**, **Picture**, **ClipArt**. Select appropriate shape. Encourage students to look for outlines of subject.

Step 5: Stretch the image to be as large as the slide. To maintain the original proportions, press **Shift** while dragging one of the corner sizing handles.

Step 6: Go to **View**, **Slide Sorter**. This option is also available as an icon (4 squares) on the bottom left of the PowerPoint screen.

Step 7: Be sure to be in the slide sorter view. **Select** the first slide. Go to **Insert**, select **Duplicate Slide**. Repeat this to get as many blank pages of the shape as needed.

Step 8: Go back to slide view and begin to add information. **Insert**, **Text Box**.

Step 9: Go to **View**, **Toolbars**, select **Drawing**. Next, select text box (click on outside edge of box), and **Down Arrow** on the **Line Color** icon (paintbrush) on the Drawing toolbar. Select **No Line** option.

Step 10: Go to **File**, **Print**. Cut out shapes and fasten together.

figure **1.60**

figure **1.61**

figure **1.62**   figure **1.63**

figure **1.64**

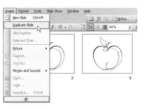

figure **1.65**

figure **1.66**

Information Literacy Standards for Student Learning

The student who is information literate uses information accurately and creatively.

The student who is an independent learner is information literate and appreciates literature and other creative expressions of information.

NETS Standards:

Students are proficient in the use of technology.

Students demonstrate a sound understanding of the nature and operation of technology systems.

Students use technology tools to process data and report results.

"SOUPER" REPORT
Clever book report idea!

Task Description: Students will prepare a book report using a standard sized soup can for the base of the report. Creating a book report in this manner is a big hit with younger students especially when they figure out that not as much information will fit on the soup label as on a traditional report. This is a super (or souper) project.

I. PLAN

Curricular Connections:

> *Book reports, fiction or nonfiction.*

> *Project reports – think of the possibilities.*

> *Creative writing projects, poetry, limericks.*

> *Research about any topic can be "Souper" reported.*

> *Donate soup cans to a food pantry when the projects are not on display anymore.*

Grade levels: K-6

Subject Areas:

> *Elective Areas*

> *Language Arts*

> *Library*

> *Science*

> *Social Studies*

Software: Word

II. PREPARE

> ❑ *Decide topics to be studied.*

> ❑ *Prepare a schedule for each student, if necessary, based on number of computers available.*

> ❑ *Practice setting margins in Word.*

> ❑ *Practice inserting text boxes and wrapping text around images.*

> ❑ *Experiment with finished size of project, depending upon size of can.*

III. PRESENT

Step 1: Discuss topics for "Souper" report and how students need to select and edit information carefully, so that it fits on a soup can. Display samples.

Step 2: Demonstrate how to change margins in Word, find images, insert text boxes, and the text-wrapping feature.

Step 3: Open **Word**, **File**, **New**. Go to **File**, **Page Setup**. Change **Margins**. Measurements given are for a standard soup can. Adjust, if need be.
Top 0.2 inches
Bottom 7.3 inches
Left 0.4 inches
Right 0.4 inches
If pop up appears stating that one or more margins are outside of printable area, click **Ignore**.

Step 4: Go to **View**, select **Ruler**. Look at the rulers to determine where the text will go.

Step 5: Go to **Insert**, select **Text box**. Add information. Type title and report in a size 12 font.

Step 6: Go to **Insert**, **Picture**, **ClipArt**. Insert ClipArt images.

Step 7: **Right click** on the outside border of the text box.

Step 8: Select **Format Textbox**, **Layout** tab, choose **Tight**. Text will wrap tightly around the text box.

Step 9: On **Drawing** toolbar (go to **View**, **Toolbars**, and **Drawing**), select **Line Color** icon (paintbrush), **Down Arrow** and choose **No Line**.

Step 10: **File**, **Print** report. Measure the can size and cut paper accordingly. Tape onto can.

figure **1.67**

figure **1.68**

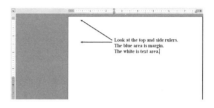

figure **1.69**

figure **1.70**

figure **1.71**

3x3 Post-It® Notes

Best Fishes

Information Literacy Standards for Student Learning

The student who is information literate uses information accurately and creatively.

The student who is an independent learner is information literate and appreciates literature and other creative expressions of information.

NETS Standards:

Students are proficient in the use of technology.

Students develop positive attitudes toward technology uses that support lifelong learning, collaboration, personal pursuits, and productivity.

Students use technology tools to enhance learning, increase productivity, and promote creativity.

3 x 3 POST-IT® NOTES
Learning how to print these notes is fun, creative, and useful!

Task Description: With this project, students will discover a great way to communicate ideas. Printing Post-It® notes is great fun and a project that children of all ages enjoy. Make sure to save the first page that you print for the placement and printing of future notes. This project is guaranteed to be well liked by students of all ages.

I. PLAN

Curricular Connections:

Labeling any project.

Labels for display purposes.

Communicating needs and ideas.

Fun, fun, fun!

Grade levels: All

Subject Areas: All

Software: PowerPoint

II. PREPARE

❑ *Decide subject matter of notes.*

❑ *Prepare a schedule for each student, if necessary, based on number of computers available.*

❑ *Practice changing page setup and margins in PowerPoint.*

❑ *Practice rotation of text in PowerPoint.*

❑ *View and understand the printing options in PowerPoint.*

❑ *Have a ready supply of 3 x 3 Post-it® notes.*

III. PRESENT

Step 1: Discuss subject of notes.

Step 2: Demonstrate how to create and print Post-it® notes. Display samples. Emphasize the importance of selecting the correct print option.

Step 3: Open **PowerPoint, File, Blank Presentation, Blank Slide.**

Step 4: Go to **File**, **Page Setup**. Change **Width to 7.5 inches**. (Height is already 7.5 inches.)

Step 5: Go to **Insert**, **Picture**, add **WordArt**, **ClipArt** images; vary the text fonts and colors. Create four full sized slides. Each slide will print as one Post-it® note. Encourage creativity because this is really fun!

Step 6: Go to **File**, **Print**, **Print What – Handouts**, **4 per page**. Check **Frame Slides**.
Print one page.

Step 7: **Place Post-it® notes over the existing printed images.**

Step 8: Go to **File**, **Print**, *underline* _uncheck_ **Frame Slides**.

Step 9: With same settings, (**Print**, **Handouts**, **4 per page**), **Print** again with the Post-it® notes on the page.

figure **1.72**

figure **1.73**

figure **1.74**

figure **1.75**

figure **1.76**

Front of trading card...

figure **1.77**

Back...

Great Grandma, Carrie, Bryn and Annaliese traveled by train to New York City.

They had lunch at a famous doll store and spent the afternoon shopping.

Bryn brought Annaliese with her that day! She got to buy some new outfits for her doll and left Aunt Wynn's doll in the doll hospital to get new hair.

A great time was had by all!

Information Literacy Standards for Student Learning

The student who is information literate accesses information efficiently and effectively.

The student who is an independent learner is information literate and strives for excellence in information seeking and knowledge generation.

The student who is information literate uses information accurately and creatively.

NETS Standards:

Students are proficient in the use of technology.

Students demonstrate a sound understanding of the nature and operation of technology systems.

Students use technology tools to enhance learning, increase productivity, and promote creativity.

TRADING CARDS
Who doesn't enjoy trading cards?

Task Description: Trading cards are not just for baseball players anymore. Students have examples of famous people all around them, in every subject area. This project encourages students to think about what makes a person famous. Concise language is required due to the limited space available. Good trading cards also make use of photographs or images. Publishing trading cards is a way to advertise upcoming events, promote new books, and write biography reports. The possibilities are endless.

I. PLAN

Curricular Connections:

   Library - authors of students' favorite books.

   Language Arts - author studies of books read in class or for book reports.

   Creative writing project introducing hero or favorite person.

   Math, Science, Social Studies - studies of famous people.

Grade levels: 3-8

Subject Areas: All

Software: Word

II. PREPARE

❑ *Introduce topics and display trading cards, both commercially made and student made.*

❑ *Prepare a schedule for each student, if necessary, based on number of computers available.*

❑ *Practice changing margins in Word.*

❑ *Practice changing Page Setup in Word.*

❑ *Practice inserting columns in Word.*

❑ *Find good sources for images for trading cards. www.pics4learning.com is a source for free images.*

❑ *Prepare a review of copyright issues about using online images.*

III. PRESENT

Step 1: Discuss topics with students. Display trading cards and discuss the information that is found on the cards. Information can include the person's name, a photo of the person, important dates and significant life events, a quote by the person, and any other information vital to the project.

Step 2: Demonstrate the techniques and skills needed in Word.

Step 3: Open **Word**, **File**, **New**, **Blank document**.

Step 4: Go to **File**, **Page Setup**, **Margins** tab, **change all margins to .25 inches**. When Pop-up regarding margins appears, select **Ignore**.

Step 5: Go to **File**, **Page Setup**, **Paper** tab, change **Width** to **6 inches** and **Height** to **4 inches**.

Step 6: Go to **Format**, **Columns**. Choose **Two**. The first column is the front of the card; the second column is the back. Create the card including all required information. Experiment with WordArt, ClipArt, and images.

Step 7: Go to **File**, **Print**. Print on cardstock and laminate for durability. Cut the cards to four by six inches. Fold in half and glue together.

figure **1.78**

figure **1.79**

figure **1.80**

figure **1.81**

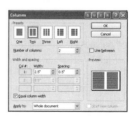

figure **1.82**

Witches on broomsticks
Ghosts
Howling wind
Full moon
Costumes
Trick or Treat
Goblins
Scary
Spooky

Halloween

Information Literacy Standards for Student Learning

The student who is information literate uses information accurately and creatively.

The student who is an independent learner is information literate and appreciates literature and other creative expressions of information.

NETS Standards:

Students are proficient in the use of technology.

Students use technology tools to enhance learning, increase productivity, and promote creativity.

TREE MAPS

Let a picture of a tree represent the season of the year, adding descriptive vocabulary to the branches!

Task Description: Students will create a graphic organizer using a tree and its branches. The trunk of the tree represents the main idea, while the branches hold descriptive words about the topic. This project adapts well to every season of the year.

I. PLAN

Curricular Connections:

Graphic organizer for creative writing or reports.

Study of synonyms.

Poetry project, follow the seasons of the year with the tree's cycle.

Study of parts of speech.

Grade Levels: 2-6

Subject Areas: Language Arts

Software: PowerPoint

II. PREPARE

❏ *Choose topics for assignment.*

❏ *Prepare a schedule for each student, if necessary, based on number of computers available.*

❏ *Practice inserting ClipArt in PowerPoint.*

❏ *Experiment with text boxes in PowerPoint.*

III. PRESENT

Step 1: Introduce the idea of tree map. Assign the topic and display samples.

Step 2: Demonstrate how to insert ClipArt and add text boxes.

Step 3: Open **PowerPoint**, **File**, **New**, **Blank presentation**, **Blank slide**.

Step 4: Go to **Insert**, **Picture**, **ClipArt**. Find the perfect tree and insert it into the slide.

Step 5: Stretch the image, filling the slide. To maintain the original proportions, press Shift while dragging one of the corner sizing handles.

Step 6: Go to **Insert**, **Text Box**. Add information to the trunk and branches.

Step 7: To rotate text box, select image. **Click** on the **green** circle and turn the text box.

Step 8: Go to **File**, **Print**, and display.

figure **1.83**

figure **1.84**

figure **1.85**

figure **1.86**

Information Literacy Standards for Student Learning

The student who is information literate uses information accurately and creatively.

The student who is information literate accesses information efficiently and effectively.

NETS Standards:

Students are proficient in the use of technology.

Students use technology tools to enhance learning, increase productivity, and promote creativity.

T-SHIRTS
Great fun for bulletin board displays and contests!

Task Description: Students will design a T-shirt. The front of the shirt will have a table with information about the topic and the back is filled with images. Students will print, tape, glue, or staple the pages together and then cut into the T-shirt shape. What a display these shirts make! If your budget allows, buy transfer paper, print the students' designs, and iron onto real T-shirts. Students love this project, especially if they can wear the finished creations.

I. PLAN

Curricular Connections:

Country or state reports.

Culture reports.

Inventors and inventions.

Biographical information.

Grade levels: 3-8

Subject Areas: All

Software: PowerPoint

II. PREPARE

❑ *Discuss topics and show students samples.*

❑ *Prepare a schedule for each student, if necessary, based on number of computers available.*

❑ *Practice changing orientation in PowerPoint.*

❑ *Practice working with a table in PowerPoint.*

❑ *Practice importing and arranging graphics in PowerPoint.*

❑ *Provide sites where students can find images suitable to their projects. Try www.pics4learning.com for free images.*

❑ *Prepare a review of copyright information regarding fair use of images.*

III. PRESENT

Step 1: Introduce, discuss project requirements, and display T-shirts.

Step 2: Demonstrate PowerPoint techniques.

Step 3: Open **PowerPoint**, go to **File**, **New**, **Blank Presentation**, and select **Blank Slide**.

Step 4: Go to **File**, **Page Setup**, and select **Portrait**.

Step 5: Go to **Format**, **Slide Layout**, and select **Title and Table** for the first slide with the information. Insert **WordArt** for title

Step 6: **Double click** on the **table** icon on the slide. A good fit is three columns by four rows. Click **OK**.

Step 7: Add information to the table. Remind students to leave two to three inches at the top of each page for the "neckline" cutout.

Step 8: Slide 2, go to **Format**, **Slide Layout**, and select **Blank Slide**. Again, leave two to three inches at the top of each page for the "neckline" cutout.

Step 9: Add information with WordArt, graphics, different font colors, types. Insert images or photographs. Remind students of copyright issues.

Step 10: Go to **File**, **Print** pages. Tape or glue together. Cut out a neckline and the sleeve area.

figure **1.87**

figure **1.88**

figure **1.89**

figure **1.90** figure **1.91**

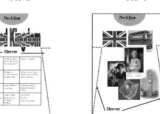

Chapter Two
Publish and Present

The finished products of the lessons in Chapter 2 will be printed ones. Students will prepare their work in Word or PowerPoint and upon completion will have a project to hand in and to share with classmates. These projects will not only provide you with incredible bulletin boards and displays but will also engage students in higher-level thinking. The lessons in Chapter 2 can be adapted to all age groups and curricula. As always, you are the best judge of where, when, and how you might be able to use and adapt the ideas.

As with the lessons in Chapter 1, the publishing project directions are written in a step-by-step manner to make it as easy as possible for you to follow and to instruct. Scheduling computer time or the number of students per group is a task that will need to be done before your class begins. Try some random methods of grouping for these publishing projects or create the groups however best suits you and your class. Ask for volunteers for helping with the projects. Teach these students first and then let each of them teach their groups. The student helpers are happy, other students accept advice from them, and you will maintain a reasonable semblance of sanity. You might even be fortunate enough to have parent volunteers who would be willing to help.

Good luck with the printed projects. Students will publish high-quality reports that will amaze and astound you. Let the publishing begin!

Adams Twelve Five Star Schools
Rocky Mountain Elementary School
3350 W. 99th Ave.
Westminster, Colorado 80030

figure **2.1**

L is for... LADYBUG

Ladybug - small round bright colored and spotted beetle that usually feeds on aphids and other insect pests. Family Coccinellidae.

Part of speech: Noun

Synonyms: lady beetle, ladybeetle, ladybird, ladybird beetle

Interesting fact: In many places in Europe, tradition says you get a wish granted if a ladybug lands on you!

Second meaning: Ladybug is an arcade game made by Universal Games and released in 1981.

Information & Image from: Wikipedia.com

Information Literacy Standards for Student Learning

The student who is information literate accesses information efficiently and effectively.

The student who is information literate uses information accurately and creatively.

NETS Standards:

Students are proficient in the use of technology.

Students use technology tools to enhance learning, increase productivity, and promote creativity.

Students use technology tools to process data and report results.

A IS FOR ...
Dictionary entries even Webster would like!

Task Description: Students will be researching and creating dictionary pages. Each student is assigned a letter to work on and then add to a group book or each student can produce an entire alphabet of words, meanings, and sentences. You decide how this project will best serve the needs of your class.

I. PLAN

Curricular Connections:

New vocabulary words with definitions.

Foreign language vocabulary with definitions.

Vocabulary for any subject, any unit of study.

Vocabulary for literature.

Glossary for reports.

Grade levels: All

Subject Areas: All

Software: Word

II. PREPARE

❑ *Decide the topics to be studied and how many letters of the alphabet each child will be assigned. Set the requirements for project. Do you want multiple meanings, images, sentences, pronunciations, and parts of speech included in the dictionary page?*

❑ *Prepare a schedule for each student, if necessary, based on number of computers available.*

❑ *Practice changing margins in Word.*

❑ *Practice adding a border, WordArt, ClipArt, and text boxes.*

❑ *Find online dictionaries for students to use. Try www.refdesk.com.*

❑ *Have print dictionaries available for students.*

III. PRESENT

Step 1: Introduce the idea of creating dictionary pages. Explain the parameters of the assignment.

Step 2: Demonstrate the skills needed in Word.

Step 3: Open **Word**. Go to **File**, **New**, **Blank Document**.

Step 4: Go to **File**, **Page Setup**. Change **Margins** to **1.0** all around.

Step 5: Go to **Format**, **Borders and Shading**. Select **Borders**, then **Page Border** tab. Select the "**Box**" option and find a fun border in the Art option!

Step 6: Go to **Insert**, **WordArt**. Type in letter and word assigned or chosen.

Step 7: **Insert** additional **Text Boxes** to add the word, part of speech, synonyms, interesting facts, whatever is required for the assignment.

Step 8: Go to **Format**, **Toolbars**, and select **Drawing** toolbar. Right click on the outside of the text box. **Select** the **Line Color** icon (paintbrush), down arrow and select **No Line**. Get creative adding images to help other students visualize that word.

Step 9: Go to **File**, **Print**. Combine the class projects into one dictionary.

figure **2.2**

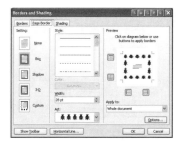

figure **2.3**

figure **2.4**

Heavy rains & high velocity winds blowing circularly around eye of storm

Usual path…northwesterly direction then northeast (northern hemisphere)

Radar used to supply weather forecasting

Ranges of wind 74mph –above 155mph

Intensity of wind speed measured by Saffir-Simpson Scale of 1-5 (strongest = 5)

Circular direction of wind around low pressure center (eye of storm)

Atmospheric pressure drops as wind velocity rises

Names - World Meteorological Organization uses six lists in rotation. New name is added if a hurricane is very deadly or costly.

Equatorial belt having doldrums (intermittent calm seas, light breezes and frequent squalls)

Information Literacy Standards for Student Learning

The student who is information literate uses information accurately and creatively.

The student who is an independent learner is information literate and appreciates literature and other creative expressions of information.

NETS Standards:

Students are proficient in the use of technology.

Students use technology tools to enhance learning, increase productivity, and promote creativity.

Students use technology tools to process data and report results.

ACROSTIC RESEARCH
Experiment with a different type of puzzle!

Task Description: Constructing an acrostic adds interest to research. Students will take the name of a person, place, or thing and find something about it that begins with each of its letters. Done in PowerPoint, this project is visually pleasing and graphically fun. The finished products make an interesting display.

I. PLAN

Curricular Connections:

Science projects, animals, weather, minerals, chemicals.

Biographical information about historical figure.

Geography and social studies places and events.

Mathematicians, who are they and what did they do?

Authors, who are they and what did they write?

Literary characters, who are they and what did they do in the book?

Grade levels: 3-8

Subject Areas: All

Software: PowerPoint

II. PREPARE

❑ *Decide topics for research.*

❑ *Prepare a schedule for each student, if necessary, based on number of computers available.*

❑ *Practice changing orientation of page in PowerPoint.*

❑ *Practice using WordArt in PowerPoint.*

❑ *Practice inserting an image into WordArt.*

❑ *Practice inserting and positioning text boxes.*

III. PRESENT

Step 1: Introduce the project. Explain that an acrostic is a type of a puzzle. Display samples.

Step 2: Demonstrate in PowerPoint how to use WordArt, change page setup, insert and use WordArt and text boxes.

Step 3: Open **PowerPoint**, **File**, **New Presentation**, **Blank Slide**.

Step 4: Go to **File**, **Page Setup**, and select **Portrait**.

Step 5: Go to **Insert**, **Picture**, **WordArt**. Select the first WordArt in the dialog box. It is plain and has no fill. Type the person, place, or thing being researched in all capital letters.

Step 6: Go to the Drawing toolbar and select **WordArt Vertical Text**. Once text is changed to vertical, pull on any of the **handles** of the WordArt to **stretch** it to fill the left hand side of the page.

Step 7: To add text for each letter, go to **Insert**, **Text Box**. Enter a new text box for each letter of the acrostic. Add the researched information.

Step 8: Add an image to the WordArt. For example, a picture of a rainbow if that is the topic. The student must first **find** and **save** an **image** to **My Picture file.**

Step 9: **Right click** on the **WordArt**. Select **Format WordArt**, then **Colors and Lines**. Option of **Fill**, look for **Color**, and use the **down arrow**. Choose **Fill Effects**, **Picture** tab, click on Select Picture. Find the image and click Insert. Then click OK and OK again on the next screen. The image will now be the **fill** of the WordArt.

Step 10: Go to **File**, **Print**, and display the finished products.

figure **2.5**

figure **2.6**

figure **2.7**

figure **2.8**

Front

FLASH CARDS
Every teacher uses flash cards!

Task Description: Flash cards can be used effectively for so many classes. Students can review vocabulary, number facts, shapes, and so much more. Students will create this project in PowerPoint. As an added benefit, they will be reviewing the material while making the flash cards.

I. PLAN

Curricular Connections:

Sight words and meanings.

Nonfiction convention terms, such as index, caption, glossary, table of contents, labels, photographs, text types, photographs, cutaways, maps, charts, tables.

Genre definitions, science fiction, mystery, folk tales, fairy tales, and more.

Unit of study vocabulary and definition or image.

Shape names and pictures for the younger students or ELL students.

Color words and color.

International language words and translations.

Number facts.

Grade levels: All

Subject Areas: All

Software: PowerPoint

II. PREPARE

❑ *Decide topic to be reviewed with flashcards.*

❑ *Prepare a schedule for each student, if necessary, based on number of computers available.*

❑ *Discover Page Setup in PowerPoint. Note where to change the orientation to portrait.*

❑ *Practice reading the Print dialog box. Print what? Handouts, four per page.*

❑ *Practice inserting text boxes and images, changing fonts and colors.*

III. PRESENT

Step 1: Introduce the flash card project. Display some of your students' or your own creations. Encourage originality in design.

Step 2: Demonstrate techniques in PowerPoint, such as Page Setup, Print dialog box, text boxes and anything else your students need to learn or review.

Step 3: Open **PowerPoint**. Go to **File**, **New Presentation**, **Blank Slide**.

Step 4: Go to **File**, **Page Setup**, and select **Portrait**.

Step 5: Go to **Insert**, **Text Box**. Add flash card information. Each slide is one side of one flash card. Make the text as large as possible and if images are added, make sure they fill the slide.

Step 6: Go to **File**, **Print**. Find **Print what** in dialog box and **down arrow** to **Handouts**. **Down Arrow** to **Four per page**. Print pages. Cut the flash cards apart and tape or glue together. Laminate for extra durability. If larger flash cards are needed, print as **Handouts**, **Two per page**.

figure **2.9**

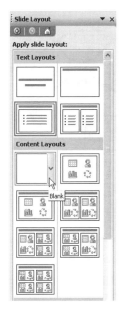

figure **2.10**

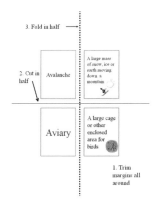

figure **2.11**

Information Literacy Standards for Student Learning

The student who is information literate uses information accurately and creatively.

The student who is information literate evaluates information critically and competently.

NETS Standards:

Students are proficient in the use of technology.

Students use technology tools to enhance learning, increase productivity, and promote creativity.

GO FOR THE GOAL
Join a research and writing project with sports activities. It is a winning combination!

Task Description: Students will write descriptively and creatively with this activity. Their writing is inserted into the shape of a soccer ball, football, baseball, or other sports equipment shape. You will find out who the budding journalists are in your classes. Who can fit the who, what, when, where, why, and maybe how of a news story into a specific shape?

I. PLAN

Curricular Connections:

Newspaper unit.

Book report.

Sports report.

Creative writing activity.

Sports vocabulary.

Grade levels: 3-8

Subject Areas:

Elective Classes

Language Arts

Library

Software: PowerPoint

II. PREPARE

❑ *Decide topics to be researched.*

❑ *Prepare a schedule for each student, if necessary, based on number of computers available.*

❑ *Practice inserting graphics into PowerPoint.*

❑ *Practice inserting text boxes and grouping text boxes and images.*

III. PRESENT

Step 1: Discuss the project with students and show examples.

Step 2: Demonstrate how to find and insert ClipArt, how to enlarge the ClipArt to fill the slide, and how to use Text Boxes.

Step 3: Open **PowerPoint**. Go to **File**, **New**, **Blank Presentation**, and **Blank Slide**.

Step 4: Go to **Insert**, **Picture**, **ClipArt**. Search for a soccer ball, baseball, football, hockey stick, ice skates; whatever image suits the project. Select a basic ClipArt image that will provide more writing area.

Step 5: Go to **Insert**, **Text Box**. Add text to the various portions of the image. Students' writing has to be concise and well planned to fit the information in small spaces.

Step 6: When finished adding text, group all of the text boxes and the image. Hold the Shift key down while selecting each text box and image. On **Drawing Toolbar**, **Down Arrow** at Draw and choose **Group**.

Step 7: Go to **File**, **Print**. Display the creative results.

figure **2.12**

figure **2.13**

figure **2.14**

figure **2.15**

Airy, pretty wings
Orange and black butterfly
Flies gracefully by

Information Literacy Standards for Student Learning

The student who is information literate uses information accurately and creatively.

The student who is an independent learner is information literate and appreciates literature and other creative expressions of information.

NETS Standards:

Students are proficient in the use of technology.

Students use technology tools to enhance learning, increase productivity, and promote creativity.

HAIKU
This is an elegant and artistic project!

Task Description: This project fosters an appreciation of the ancient form of Japanese poetry. Haiku is a powerful form of expression and makes a wonderful display. Using PowerPoint, students capture the essence of haiku in imagery and original verse. Have students create a banner explaining the elements of haiku.

I. PLAN

Curricular Connections:

Language Arts

Creative Writing Project

Grade levels: 6-12

Subject Areas: Language Arts

Software: PowerPoint

II. PREPARE

❑ *Decide parameters of subject matter, if any.*

❑ *Provide a list of Web sites about haiku. Suggestions:*

http://www.ahapoetry.com/haiku.htm

http://www.toyomasu.com/haiku/

http://www.hsa-haiku.org/

❑ *Have haiku books available for students to use.*

❑ *Prepare a schedule for each student, if necessary, based on number of computers available.*

❑ *Practice importing an image into PowerPoint. Practice changing that image to washout.*

❑ *Practice inserting a text box, changing font sizes, colors, and removing the outside line of the text box.*

III. PRESENT

Step 1: Discuss the elements of haiku; emphasize the basic five-seven-five syllable structure, and the idea of capturing a simple moment eloquently. Read and display examples.

Step 2: Demonstrate techniques required in PowerPoint; techniques of inserting an image, making it a washout (watermark), inserting a text box, and any other skill that needs to be reviewed.

Step 3: Open **PowerPoint**. Go to **File**, **New**, **Blank Presentation**. Go to **Format**, **Slide Layout**, and select **Blank Slide**.

Step 4: Go to **Insert**, **Picture**, **ClipArt**. Pull on one of the four corner handles of the clipart to re-size it to fill the slide.

Step 5: **Right click** on the **ClipArt** image. Select **Format Picture**, **Picture** tab. Find **Image Control**, **Color**. **Down Arrow** to **Washout**. Click **OK**. Experiment with changing the brightness or contrast.

Step 6: Go to **Insert**, **Text Box**. Place text box on top of graphic. Type in haiku, changing font, font color, and font sizes.

Step 7: To make sure the text does not move, hold the **Shift** key down while selecting text box and image. On **Drawing Toolbar**, **Down Arrow** at **Draw** and choose **Group**.

Step 8: Go to **File**, **Print**.

figure **2.16**

figure **2.17**

figure **2.18**

LOOPING PAPER CHAINS
Students of all ages enjoy this hands-on project!

Task Description: Students will create paper chains in PowerPoint. This is a hands-on activity that is excellent for book reports, explaining sequential events, and having fun! Students will have a great time, not only creating their projects but displaying them as well.

Information Literacy Standards for Student Learning

The student who is information literate uses information accurately and creatively.

The student who is an independent learner is information literate and strives for excellence in information seeking and knowledge generation.

NETS Standards:

Students are proficient in the use of technology.

Students use technology tools to enhance learning, increase productivity, and promote creativity.

I. PLAN

Curricular Connections:

Sequential learning tasks.

Creative writing projects.

Art and science project … how does that caterpillar move along?

Grade levels: K-6

Subject Areas:

Language Arts

Library

Science

Software: PowerPoint

II. PREPARE

❑ *Decide topics.*

❑ *Prepare a schedule for each student, if necessary, based on number of computers available.*

❑ *Practice working in PowerPoint, including importing graphics and text boxes.*

❑ *Understand the options in the Print Dialog box.*

❑ *Learn how to duplicate a slide in PowerPoint*

III. PRESENT

Step 1: Introduce topic and display example of paper chain projects.

Step 2: Demonstrate various techniques needed in PowerPoint.

Step 3: Open **PowerPoint**. Go to **File**, **New**, **Blank Presentation**.

Step 4: Go to **File**, **Page Setup**. Change **Height** to 5 inches.

Step 5: Go to **Insert**, **New Slide**. Select which layout works best for the project. Add text and graphics, filling the individual slides.

Step 6: Go to **View**, **Slide Sorter**. The Slide Sorter option is found in the drop down menu or on the drawing toolbar. On the drawing toolbar, it is represented by four squares (slides) together.

Step 7: **Select** first slide. Go to **Insert**, **Duplicate Slide**. Repeat with each slide. Keep project in Slide Sorter view.

Step 8: Go to **File**, **Print**, **Print What**, **Handouts**, **6 per page.** Select **Frame Slide** option.

Step 9: Cut the strips across. Staple, glue, or tape paper chains together. Add a plain paper chain between the printed ones for greater flexibility.

figure **2.19**

figure **2.20**

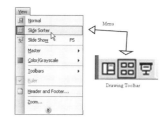

figure **2.21**

figure **2.22**

figure **2.23**

Information Literacy Standards for Student Learning

The student who is information literate uses information accurately and creatively.

The student who is an independent learner is information literate and appreciates literature and other creative expressions of information.

NETS Standards:

• Students demonstrate a sound understanding of the nature and operation of technology systems.

Students use technology tools to enhance learning, increase productivity, and promote creativity.

MINI GIFT BAGS
Put business envelopes to good use!

Task Description: Students will design Mini Gift Bags out of #10 business-sized envelopes. The amount of information and images that fit on an envelope is limited but it is a great presentation tool.

I. PLAN

Curricular Connections:

Create gift bags for small items.

"What's in the bag?" guessing game.

Research project similar to Bag Tags in Chapter 1 – label what is inside the bag.

Grade levels: 3-12

Subject Areas: All

Software: Word

II. PREPARE

❏ *Decide topic to be studied and displayed on and in gift bags.*

❏ *Prepare a schedule for each student, if necessary, based on number of computers available.*

❏ *Practice changing orientation in Word page setup.*

❏ *Experiment with how different printers work. Does the envelope go into the printer with its flap down or flap up?*

❏ *Practice cutting, folding, and shaping the gift bag.*

III. PRESENT

Step 1: Discuss and introduce topic and idea of making mini gift bags. Display samples.

Step 2: Review techniques needed in Word.

Step 3: Open **Word**. **File**, **New**, **Blank Document**.

Step 4: Go to **File**, **Page Setup**. Select **Paper** tab, **down arrow** at **Paper Size** to **Envelope #10**.

Step 5: **View**, select **Ruler**.

Step 6: Add text, clip art, graphics; make it creative and fun. Make sure that the information and images are in the bottom half of the text area.

Step 7: Go to **File**, **Print**. Cut off the top of envelope. Fold sides and bottoms into the center and crease. Glue or tape the corner pieces to the bottom of the bag.

figure **2.24**

figure **2.25**

figure **2.26**

figure **2.27**

Information Literacy Standards for Student Learning

The student who is information literate accesses information efficiently and effectively.

The student who is information literate uses information accurately and creatively.

NETS Standards:

Students demonstrate a sound understanding of the nature and operation of technology systems.

Students are proficient in the use of technology.

Students use technology tools to enhance learning, increase productivity, and promote creativity.

OVER THE TOP
A slightly different version of a pop-up book!

Task Description: Students will produce a project in a very different format. Instead of a pop-up book, this is a "pop-over" book. This lesson is creative, hands-on, and enjoyable. Students will practice their listening skills as well as their fine motor skills. The finished products make a great bulletin board. Title it: "We're over the top about …" and make an Excel banner to promote the students' work.

I. PLAN

Curricular Connections:

Research and report on animals, vegetables, minerals, people, places, and things.

Creative writing project.

Poetry, haiku, limericks.

Art project.

Grade levels: K-6

Subject Areas:

Electives

Language Arts

Library

Science

Software: PowerPoint

II. PREPARE

❑ *Decide the topic to be studied.*

❑ *Prepare a schedule for each student, if necessary, based on number of computers available.*

❑ *Practice changing page orientation in PowerPoint.*

❑ *Experiment with drawing rectangles, adding ClipArt, working within text boxes and using WordArt.*

❑ *Design, print, and fold samples.*

III. PRESENT

Step 1: Introduce topics to be covered and display samples.

Step 2: Instruct students in the techniques needed in PowerPoint.

Step 3: Open **PowerPoint**, **New**, **Blank Presentation**, **Blank Slide**.

Step 4: Go to **File**, **Page Setup**. Change Orientation to **Portrait**.

Step 5: **View**, select **Ruler** option.

Step 6: Go to **Insert**, **Picture**, **ClipArt**. Find an image that will be able to "peek over" the top of the text box. Position ClipArt in the top section of the page.

Step 7: Draw a rectangle by clicking on the rectangle icon on the drawing toolbar.

Step 8: Go to **Insert**, **Text Box** and add information.

Step 9: Go to **File**, **Print** and cut out. Fold the bottom of the box to the top of the box. Cut slits around the portion of the image hanging "into" the text box area.

Step 10: Go to **Insert**, select **Blank Slide**. Add the title of the project and student's name in top **3 inches** of slide. **Print** and cut. Glue to the front of the Over the Top book.

figure **2.28**

figure **2.29**

figure **2.30**

figure **2.31**

figure **2.32**

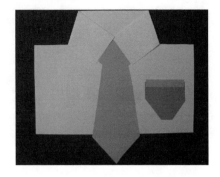

Information Literacy Standards for Student Learning

The student who is information literate accesses information efficiently and effectively.

The student who is information literate uses information accurately and creatively.

NETS Standards:

Students demonstrate a sound understanding of the nature and operation of technology systems.

Students are proficient in the use of technology.

Students use technology tools to enhance learning, increase productivity, and promote creativity.

SHIRT 'N TIE BOOKS
Cut and paste a shirt and tie, or blouse and bow!

Task Description: Students will have fun creating this report. With a 12 x 18 inch sheet of construction paper, they will measure, cut, fold, and add text and a great project will be the result.

I. PLAN

Curricular Connections:

Creative writing projects.

Report or research papers.

Poetry, haiku, limericks projects.

Bulletin board display - "Keep your shirt on" or "Tie these ideas together".

Grade levels: 2-6

Subject Areas:

Language Arts

Electives

Library

Software: Word

II. PREPARE

❑ *Decide topics for student projects.*

❑ *Prepare a schedule for each student, if necessary, based on number of computers available.*

❑ *Practice measuring, cutting, and folding the shirts.*

❑ *Practice changing margins, inserting a text box, graphics, WordArt in Word.*

III. PRESENT

Step 1: Introduce Shirt 'n Tie project to the students. Display samples.

Step 2: Demonstrate skills needed in Word. Demonstrate the folding, cutting, and creating of the shirt or blouse.

Step 3: Open **Word**. Go to **File**, **New**. Select **Blank document**.

Step 4: Go to **File**, **Page Setup**. Change **Margins** to:
Top 0.5 inches
Bottom 4.5 inches
Left 0.5 inches
Right 0.5 inches

Step 5: Add text to this page. Add Clipart, WordArt, graphics, and images.

Step 6: Go to **File**, **Print**. Print text and cut to fit the inside of the shirt.

Step 7: Prepare the shirt. Fold a 12x18 inch sheet of construction paper in half and crease. With the fold at the top, measure down 2 inches and cut two slits 3 inches long on each side.

Step 8: Fold each slit piece down and in diagonally to form the collar. Glue the collar in place. Decorate the shirt, add a colorful tie, or bow. Glue the text inside the shirt.

figure **2.33**

figure **2.34**

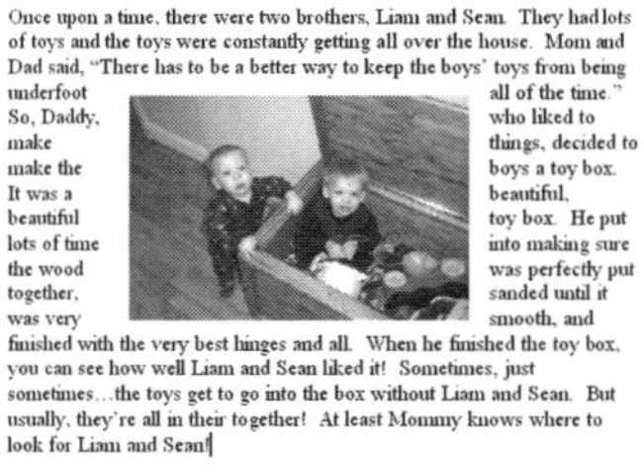

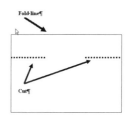

figure **2.35**

figure **2.36**

Information Literacy Standards for Student Learning

The student who is an independent learner is information literate and appreciates literature and other creative expressions of information.

The student who is information literate uses information accurately and creatively.

NETS Standards:

Students are proficient in the use of technology.

Students use technology tools to enhance learning, increase productivity, and promote creativity.

STRETCH THE STORY
Tall tales will never be the same!

Task Description: Students will have fun with this project. By changing the formatting in a Word document, a stretched-out story or a tall tale can be published! This project is fun for students to make and creates a fantastic display. Remember to make a banner for the bulletin board... How tall a tale can you tell?

I. PLAN

Curricular Connections:

Fantastic way to display tall tales.

Great bulletin board for language arts projects.

Hands-on project for genre study.

Grade levels: K-8

Subject Areas:

Language Arts

Library

Reading

Software: Word

II. PREPARE

❑ *Decide how to use the tall tale format. Will students write their own versions of tall tales?*

❑ *Prepare a schedule for each student, if necessary, based on number of computers available.*

❑ *Practice formatting in Word, creating columns, changing font sizes.*

❑ *Practice adding ClipArt and formatting the text around the ClipArt.*

III. PRESENT

Step 1: Discuss tall tales as a literature genre. Show samples of the stretched stories. Demonstrate the skills needed in Word and display samples of the project.

Step 2: Students will have written their stories and planned their illustrations before working on the computer.

Step 3: Open **Word**, Go to **File**, **New**. Select **Blank document**. Type the story.

Step 4: Go to **File**, **Page Setup**. Change **Margins** to **0.5 inches** all around.

Step 5: Go to **Format**, **Columns**. Choose **3**.

Step 6: Go to **Edit**, **Select All**. Then to **Format**, **Font**. Change the font size so that the story is two pages or more in length.

Step 7: Go to **Insert**, **Text Box**. Then to **Insert**, **Picture**, **ClipArt**. (ClipArt is much more workable if it is in a text box.) To wrap text around ClipArt, **right click** on the **text box**, select **Format Text Box**. Select the **Layout tab**. Choose **Tight**. Then click on **OK**.

Step 8: Go to **File**, **Print**. Cut the columns apart on the dotted lines and trim so that each strip is the same width. Tape or glue strips together.

figure **2.37**

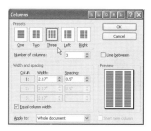

figure **2.38**

figure **2.39**

figure **2.40**

figure 2.41

Front of card

Inside of card

Information Literacy Standards for Student Learning

The student who is information literate uses information accurately and creatively.

NETS Standards:

Students are proficient in the use of technology.

Students demonstrate a sound understanding of the nature and operation of technology systems.

THANK YOU, THANK YOU, THANK YOU!
Few things please people more than receiving a thank you note!

Task Description: Students will write a thank you note to a favorite author, famous person, family member, or anyone. Creating a note card will be the challenge. Will students get a response from the author? It is a socially acceptable skill to know how to write a thank you note. Print two of each card, one to send to the person and one to keep for a display.

I. PLAN

Curricular Connections:

Thank you notes to favorite authors.

Letter writing practice.

Thank you notes for any and everything!

Grade levels: All

Subject Areas:

Language Arts

Library

Software: PowerPoint

II. PREPARE

❑ *Decide who is to be the recipient of the thank you note.*

❑ *Prepare a schedule for each student, if necessary, based on number of computers available.*

❑ *Practice changing margins in PowerPoint.*

❑ *Practice rotating graphics in PowerPoint.*

❑ *Discover how to add a hallmark to the back of the card.*

❑ *Find Web sites with publishers and author addresses.*

III. PRESENT

Step 1: Discuss thank you note protocol with students. Show samples of cards and explain the different parts of writing a note.

Step 2: Review PowerPoint techniques needed for this project.

Step 3: Open **PowerPoint**, **New**, **Blank Presentation**, **Blank Slide**.

Step 4: Go to **File**, **Page Setup**, **Margins**. Change **Width to 11 inches**, **Height to 8.5 inches**.

Step 5: Go to **View**, select **Ruler**. Draw a line across the page at mid-section (zero on the ruler) both horizontally and vertically. See Figure 2.42 for placement of the sections of the note card. (Note that the "cover" is rotated so that it appears upside down.)

Step 6: Go to **Insert**, **Textbox**. Add text to the note portion of the rectangle.

Step 7: Go to **Insert**, **Picture**, **ClipArt.** Select an image that is representative of the author's work. Drag it into the upper left hand portion of the slide, in the cover area, and rotate it by grabbing the green handle.

Step 8: Add a hallmark. **Insert**, **Picture**, **ClipArt**. Select an image that is representative of the project and drag it into the lower left hand corner of the slide. **Right Click** on the **ClipArt**, select **Format Picture**. Find the **Image Control**, **Color**, **Down Arrow** to **Washout**. Click **OK**.

Step 9: Go to **Insert**, **Text Box**. Add initials or name to the hallmark.

Step 10: Before printing, remove the lines dividing the card. Go to **File**, **Print**. Fold in half and in half again.

figure **2.42**

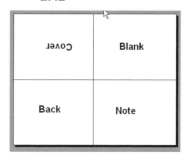

figure **2.43**

Grab the green handle and rotate the ClipArt.

figure **2.44**

figure **2.45**

Information Literacy Standards for Student Learning

The student who is information literate uses information accurately and creatively.

The student who is information literate accesses information efficiently and effectively.

NETS Standards:

Students are proficient in the use of technology.

Students use technology tools to enhance learning, increase productivity, and promote creativity.

WHAT'S IN THE WINDOW?
A new, different, and exciting way to write a report!

Task Description: Students will write a report or news story asking and answering the who, what, when, where, and why questions of good journalism. This project is creative, hands-on, and is created in PowerPoint.

I. PLAN

Curricular Connections:

Book report.

Character study.

Newspaper article.

Concise writing practice.

Grade levels: 2-8

Subject Areas:

Language Arts

Library

Reading

Software: PowerPoint

II. PREPARE

☐ *Decide the topic of study.*

☐ *Prepare a schedule for each student, if necessary, based on number of computers available.*

☐ *Practice working in PowerPoint. Experiment with inserting ClipArt, WordArt, and text.*

☐ *Review the printing procedure. It is important to print as Handouts, 6 per page.*

III. PRESENT

Step 1: Introduce topic to students. Display examples of projects.

Step 2: Review the skills in PowerPoint needed to prepare the assignment. Have students look at the print screen to see the option of printing handouts.

Step 3: Open **PowerPoint**, **New**, **Blank Presentation**, **Title Slide**, or slide layout that works best for the student.

Step 4: Add text and images to 12 slides. Go to **Insert**, **Picture**, **Clip Art** or **WordArt**. Encourage creativity and be certain that students fill the entire slide with text and images.

Step 5: Slides 1-6 will be the "who, what, when, where, why, and how" slides and will print on page 1. Slides 7-12 will be the answers to the questions and will print on page 2. Make sure the entire slide is filled with text and images.

Step 6: Go to **File**, **Print**, **Print What**, **Handouts**, **6 per page**, **Frame Slides**. Be sure to monitor this portion of the project. If not, all 12 slides will be printed full size and that is a tremendous waste of ink and paper.

Step 7: On page 1, cut around the bottom and both sides of each square. Glue page 1 to page 2. Be careful not to glue the flaps!

figure **2.47**

figure **2.48**

figure **2.49**

figure **2.50**

figure **2.51**

WORDART GRAPHICS
This is amazing and fun!

Task Description: Students will demonstrate the visual meaning of a word by inserting an image of that word in a WordArt background. This technique is exciting for students to learn and to use.

I. PLAN

Curricular Connections:

Poetry, haiku, limerick projects.

Writing exercise.

Short story illustration.

Art project.

Science or math definitions.

State or culture reports.

Hero reports.

T-shirt design, print on transfer paper and iron on a T-shirt.

Grade levels: 3 - 12

Subject Areas: All

Software: PowerPoint

II. PREPARE

❑ *Decide topic to be graphically depicted.*

❑ *Prepare a schedule for each student, if necessary, based on number of computers available.*

❑ *Practice how to use WordArt in PowerPoint.*

❑ *Experiment with adding an image to the background fill.*

❑ *Prepare a list of Web sites where students can access images or have students use images they have created and saved to their My Pictures folder.*

III. PREPARE

Step 1:   Discuss project with students and display examples.

Step 2:   Demonstrate techniques and skills needed in PowerPoint for this activity.

Step 3:   Have students search for pictures to use and save it to My Pictures folder. Explain copyright issues and how to be in copyright compliance when using images. Free images are available at www.Pics4Learning.com.

Step 4:   Open **PowerPoint**, **New**, **Blank Presentation**, **Blank Slide**.

Step 5:   Go to **Insert**, **Picture**, **WordArt**. Select a large, open design. Type word in all capital letters. Click OK.

Step 6:   **Right click** on the **WordArt**. Select **Format WordArt**.

Step 7:   On the **Colors and Lines** tab, find **Fill**, **Color**. **Down Arrow** and select the **Picture** tab.

Step 8:   Go to **Select Picture** and find the image in My Pictures file. **Select the picture** and click **OK**. Next screen, click **OK**.

Step 9:   Go to **File**, **Print** and display.

figure **2.52**

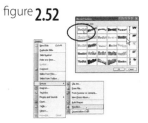

figure **2.53**

figure **2.54**

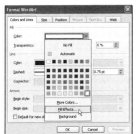

figure **2.55**

figure **2.56**

figure **2.57**

figure **2.58**

Information Literacy Standards for Student Learning

The student who is information literate uses information accurately and creatively.

The student who is an independent learner is information literate and appreciates literature and other creative expressions of information.

NETS Standards:

Students demonstrate a sound understanding of the nature and operation of technology systems.

Students use technology tools to enhance learning, increase productivity, and promote creativity.

WORDART POETRY
WOW!

Task Description: This takes WordArt to a new level. Use WordArt to create shapes and interesting backgrounds for students' writing. When printed, this project will provide an eye-catching bulletin board. Any age student can produce fantastic work.

I. PLAN

Curricular Connections:

Haiku

Poetry

Illustrations

Grade levels: 3-12

Subject Areas:

Language Arts

Library

Reading

Software: PowerPoint

II. PREPARE

❏ *Decide the topic of the poetry.*

❏ *Prepare a schedule for each student, if necessary, based on number of computers available.*

❏ *Practice using all features of the drawing toolbar in WordArt.*

❏ *Practice skills in PowerPoint.*

❏ *Experiment with resizing, editing, moving WordArt.*

III. PRESENT

Step 1: Introduce topic and display examples of WordArt poetry.

Step 2: Review and model the PowerPoint skills needed for this project.

Step 3: Open **PowerPoint**, **File**, **New**, **Blank Presentation**, **Blank Slide**.

Step 4: Go to **Insert**, **Picture**, **WordArt**. Choose WordArt style and type poem. **Suggestion: put a * between phrases**.

Step 5: **Select** the WordArt. The **Drawing Toolbar** will appear. Click on the "A" that is slanted (**WordArt Shape**). Experiment with different shapes for the poetry.

Step 6: Click and drag the poem to the center, resize and position it where it looks best.

Step 7: Go to **Insert**, **Picture**, **ClipArt**. Add images that help illustrate the poem. Resize and reposition these as needed.

Step 8: **Right click** on the **background** of the slide. Select **Background**.

Step 9: **Down Arrow** and choose **Fill Effects**. Have fun with the background options. Experiment with the different fill options. Choose one color, two colors, or presets. Click on **OK** on the Fill Effects box and then on **Apply** on the Background box.

Step 10: Go to **File**, **Print**.

figure **2.59**

figure **2.60**

figure **2.61**

figure **2.62**

figure **2.63**

Information Literacy Standards for Student Learning

The student who is information literate uses information accurately and creatively.

The student who is an independent learner is information literate and appreciates literature and other creative expressions of information.

NETS Standards:

Students demonstrate a sound understanding of the nature and operation of technology systems.

Students use technology tools to enhance learning, increase productivity, and promote creativity.

Students are proficient in the use of technology.

WRITING PAPER TEMPLATES
Letter writing is a necessary skill for students to master!

Task Description: Students will create writing paper designs for use in projects. The results can be letters, posters, signs, menus, or advertisements. Communication is an important part of advertising and a skill needed in today's workplace.

I. PLAN

Curricular Connections:

Creative writing project.

Letter to a famous person, favorite author, or relative.

Letter requesting information.

Menu.

Poetry display.

Grade levels: 3-12

Subject Areas: All

Software: PowerPoint

II. PREPARE

❑ *Decide topics to be studied.*

❑ *Prepare a schedule for each student, if necessary, based on number of computers available.*

❑ *Practice working with Page Setup in PowerPoint.*

❑ *Practice using text boxes, inserting images, and moving graphics in PowerPoint.*

III. PRESENT

Step 1: Introduce letter-writing lesson. Display examples of different writing paper samples. Discuss the need for creativity and imagination to coordinate text with images.

Step 2: Demonstrate the skills needed in PowerPoint.

Step 3: Open **PowerPoint**, **File**, **New**, **Blank Presentation.**

Step 4: Go to **File**, **Page Setup**. Change **Orientation** to **Portrait**.

Step 5: Go to **Insert**, **Picture**, **ClipArt.** Find suitable ClipArt images, borders, whatever works for the project. Insert ClipArt, and then pull on one of four corners to stretch to fill the slide.

Step 6: Go to **Insert**, **Text Box**. Add text and change fonts, font sizes, and colors.

Step 7: Go to **File**, **Print**. Print two copies, one for display, and one to send. Display letters, posters, or whatever project students created.

figure **2.64**

figure **2.65**

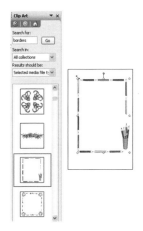

figure **2.66**

Chapter Three
Research and show what you know

Chapter 3 introduces and explains research-based technology lessons. Students will research a subject and then prepare a project in Word, Excel, or PowerPoint to publish their findings. These projects can be adapted to all age groups and curricula with the resulting products providing first-rate displays and bulletin boards. Researching a topic is a very important skill for students to have at any grade level. Use your judgment and experience to decide what projects will be most successful for your students.

The directions for all of these projects are written in a systematic, organized fashion. You will be able to practice the project, prepare samples for your students, and present to your classes with ease. Knowing how many computers are available to use is instrumental in how you set up the class and groups within the class. Students can share computers or work individually.

The research portion of the lessons is done with books, online sources, or a combination of the two. With research projects, the information and content acquired is the most important aspect of the projects. Once students have begun their research, they will be able to process the information and to display what they have learned in new and different formats. The products will be creative, informative and exciting to share. Let the research-based projects begin!

figure **3.1**

ANIMAL ALPHABET
Watch creativity blossom with this project!

Task Description: Students, either individually or in groups, will research an animal or contribute to the creation of a class book. The resulting projects will be creative and informative. Bind the pages together for a class ABC book or display individual pages on a bulletin board.

I. PLAN

Curricular Connections:

Research project about animals.

Combine all projects into a class book.

Science project - classification of animals.

Grade levers: K-8

Subject Areas:

Language Arts

Library

Science

Software: Word

II. PREPARE

❑ *Decide animals to be studied.*

❑ *Prepare a schedule for each student, if necessary, based on number of computers available.*

❑ *Find Web sites for students to experience virtual tours of zoos.*

❑ *Prepare a list of Web sites and databases for researching animals.*

❑ *Practice changing margins in Word.*

❑ *Practice inserting images.*

❑ *Experiment with changing bullet shapes.*

III. PRESENT

Step 1: Introduce and explain research project to the students. Display examples.

Step 2: Demonstrate all needed skills in Word. Provide time for research and acquisition of images into students' My Pictures files.

Step 3: Open **Word**, **File**, **New**, **Blank Document**.

Step 4: Go to **File**, **Page Setup**, **Margins** tab. **Change** margins to **0.3** inches all around. If pop-up appears advising that margins are set outside printable area click **Ignore**.

Step 5: Go to **File**, **Insert**, **Picture**, **WordArt**. Put either the initial letter or the entire animal's name in WordArt.

Step 6: Go to **Format**, **Bullets and Numbering**. Add information about the animal in bulleted list format.

Step 7: To change the bullets, make certain students have a picture or ClipArt saved to the My Pictures folder. Select the bullets. (Highlight bulleted text.) Go to **Format**, **Bullets and Numbering**, **Bulleted** tab. Click on **Customize**, **Picture**. **Select** the picture and click **OK**.

Step 8: Go to **File**, **Print**.

figure **3.2**

figure **3.3**

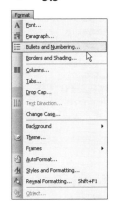

figure **3.4**

figure **3.5**

figure **3.6**

Leo
Gerstenzang

1920's

Q=Quality

Many uses

Infant
Novelty
Company
1926

Wooden
stick @ first.
Changed to
cardboard.

Information Literacy Standards for Student Learning

The student who is information literate accesses information efficiently and effectively.

The student who is information literate uses information accurately and creatively.

NETS Standards:

Students are proficient in the use of technology.

Students use technology tools to enhance learning, increase productivity, and promote creativity.

BOOKMARKS
Can you ever have enough bookmarks?

Task Description: Students will create bookmarks, with designs and information on the front and back. Designing bookmarks is a first-rate activity for contests, displays, and handouts.

I. PLAN

Curricular Connections:

Bookmarks can celebrate a season, a reason, and everything in between. Great activity for contests.

Grade levels: All

Subject Areas: All

Software: PowerPoint

II. PREPARE

❑ Decide research topics to be used.

❑ Prepare a schedule for each student, if necessary, based on number of computers available.

❑ Practice using the ruler in PowerPoint.

❑ Practice drawing rectangles and other shapes in PowerPoint.

❑ Practice copy and paste techniques in PowerPoint.

III. PRESENT

Step 1: Discuss how the research is will be displayed in a bookmark format. Hand out samples.

Step 2: Demonstrate PowerPoint skills needed to succeed and allow students research time.

Step 3: Open **PowerPoint**, **File**, **New Presentation**, **Blank Slide**.

Step 4: Go to **View**, **Ruler**. Make sure ruler option is selected and decide how large to make the bookmarks. Suggestion: **6 inches in height, 2 inches in width**. This size works well.

Step 5: Go to **View**, **Toolbars**, and select **Drawing Toolbar**. Select **AutoShapes**, **Basic Shapes**. Choose the desired shape, and click and drag it to be 6 x 2 inches.

Step 6: **Right click** on shape, **Copy. Right click, Paste**. Paste three additional shapes to create two bookmarks. Position the first and second shapes close together, leave a larger space in between, and then position the third and fourth shapes together.

Step 7: Go to **Insert**, **Text Box**. Add text. Adjust the position of the text, change font sizes, and colors. Have fun with the creation of the bookmarks.

Step 8: Go to **Insert**, **Picture**. Add interesting WordArt, ClipArt, or picture images.

Step 9: Group all objects together. Holding down the **Ctrl** key, **select** each portion of the bookmark. **Down Arrow** at **Draw** on **Drawing Toolbar**, and select **Group**.

Step 10: Go to **File**, **Print**. Cut and fold bookmarks and glue together. Laminate the bookmarks, if your budget allows.

figure **3.7**

figure **3.8**

figure **3.9**

figure **3.10**

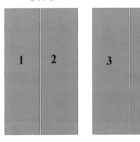

figure **3.11**

figure **3.12**

Information Literacy Standards for Student Learning

The student who is information literate uses information accurately and creatively.

The student who is an independent learner is information literate and appreciates literature and other creative expressions.

NETS Standards:

Students demonstrate a sound understanding of the nature and operation of technology systems.

Students use technology tools to enhance learning, increase productivity, and promote creativity.

BUSINESS CARDS
This project provides practice for the future!

Task Description: Students will create business cards for notable people in history. Researched information has to fit on the small card so careful editing is imperative. Adding images, ClipArt, and WordArt is a challenge within the small spaces allowed.

I. PLAN

Curricular Connections:

Business cards for famous people in history.

Business cards for infamous people in history.

Business cards for anyone, famous or infamous.

Grade levels: 4-12

Subject Areas: All

Software: Word

II. PREPARE

❏ *Select topics to be studied. Set guidelines for business card content.*

❏ *Prepare a schedule for each student, if necessary, based on number of computers available.*

❏ *Practice skills needed in Word to create projects.*

❏ *Experiment with envelopes and labels function in Word.*

❏ *Experiment with ClipArt. Practice changing the coloration to "washout," also known as a watermark.*

❏ *Practice inserting and formatting a picture so that the text wraps around the image.*

III. PRESENT

Step 1: Introduce the idea of creating business cards for notable people. Stress how small the cards really are and how concise the text has to be. Show samples.

Step 2: Review skills needed in Word to be successful. Allow students time to research and to locate images to use.

Step 3: Open **Word**, **File**, **New**, **Blank Document**.

Step 4: Go to **Tools**, **Letters and Mailings**, **Envelopes and Labels**. Down arrow to find the number for business cards, for example **Avery #8371**. If no number is available, set **Margins** to be **2 x 3.5 inches**. Click **OK**.

Step 5: Select **New Document**. Go to **Table** menu, **Show Gridlines**.

Step 6: Add text, images, quotes, information. There is not much space in a 2 x 3.5-inch area. Be sure to insert a text box and then insert an image into that text box. It is much easier to work with text and images within a text box.

Step 7: **Right Click** on **Text Box** around image. Choose **Format Text Box**. Select **Layout tab**, **Tight** option. Text will now wrap around image.

Step 8: To create a washout or watermark, select the ClipArt. Double click on it. In the Format **Picture** box, **Down Arrow** at **Color** and select Washout. Experiment with the look that will make this business card special.

Step 9: Go to **File**, **Print**. Separate the 10 cards carefully.

figure **3.13**

figure **3.14**

figure **3.15**

figure **3.16**

figure **3.17**

figure **3.18**

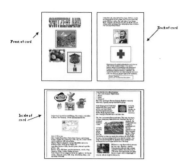

Information Literacy Standards for Student Learning

The student who is information literate accesses information efficiently and effectively.

The student who is information literate uses information accurately and creatively.

NETS Standards:

Students demonstrate a sound understanding of the nature and operation of technology systems.

Students use productivity tools to collaborate in constructing technology-enhanced models, prepare publications, and produce other creative works.

CULTURE CARDS
These cards demonstrate researched knowledge of another country and its culture!

Task Description: Students research a state, country, its geography, population, resources, other information, and display it in card format. This project encourages students to produce a graphically pleasing document. The resulting cards provide an informative display or bulletin board.

I. PLAN

Curricular Connections:

Research a country and its culture and report findings.

Holiday cards.

Cultural comparisons and contrasts.

Grade levels: 3-8

Subject Areas:

Language Arts

Library

Social Studies

Software: Word

II. PREPARE

❏ *Decide topics to be researched.*

❏ *Prepare a schedule for each student, if necessary, based on number of computers available.*

❏ *Find Web sites for students to use, databases for research available for their use.*

❏ *Practice changing margins in Word.*

❏ *Practice working within columns.*

❏ *Experiment with text boxes, formatting text and images.*

III. PRESENT

Step 1: Introduce culture cards and explain the requirements for this project. Display samples.

Step 2: Demonstrate the skills needed in Word. Allow students time to research.

Step 3: Open **Word**, **File**, **New**, **Blank Document**.

Step 4: Go to **File**, **Page Setup**, **Margins** tab. Change **Margins** to **0.5 inches** all around. Change **Orientation** to **Landscape**.

Step 5: Go to **Format**, **Columns**, and select **Two**. Select **Line Between**.

Step 6: Add text, graphics, information, WordArt, images to the card.

Step 7: Format text boxes so that the text wraps around the image. Right click on a text box surrounding an image. **Right Click** on **Text Box** around image. Choose **Format Text Box**. Select **Layout Tab**, **Tight** option. Text will now wrap around image.

Step 8: Go to **File**, **Print**. For best results, print the cards on card stock. Glue or tape pages together or print back to back, and fold on line. A second option is to cut the project into four sections, put together with a fastener in one corner, and make a flip chart.

figure **3.19**

figure **3.20**

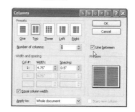

figure **3.21**

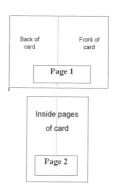

figure **3.22**

figure **3.23**

Information Literacy Standards for Student Learning

The student who is information literate evaluates information critically and competently.

The student who is an independent learner is information literate and appreciates literature and other creative expressions of information.

NETS Standards:

Students are proficient in the use of technology.

Students use technology tools to enhance learning, increase productivity, and promote creativity.

Students use technology to locate, evaluate, and collect information from a variety of sources.

EXPLAIN THIS!
Just how do things work?

Task Description: Students will research a nonfiction topic and find out how something works. The students will present their research in PowerPoint format, whether in oral presentation or printed form. This is an excellent project to display or to view. You decide which presentation format works best for your class.

I. PLAN

Curricular Connections:

Nonfiction report.

Study of inventions and inventors.

Grade levels: 3-8

Subject Areas: All

Software: PowerPoint

II. PREPARE

❑ *Decide topics of study.*

❑ *Prepare a schedule for each student, if necessary, based on number of computers available.*

❑ *Research quality Web sites and databases to suggest to students.*

❑ *Practice skills in PowerPoint, including adding graphics, text, WordArt, and images.*

❑ *Experiment with different slide layouts in PowerPoint.*

❑ *Explore different printing options PowerPoint has to offer.*

❑ *Prepare a rubric so students know what is expected and required in this project.*

III. PRESENT

Step 1: Introduce the assignment to students. Display samples of project.

Step 2: Demonstrate needed skills in PowerPoint and allow students research time.

Step 3: Open **PowerPoint**, **File**, **New**, **Blank Presentation**. Slide **Layout** of choice. Explore the options available. Scroll down to view all of the possible layouts.

Step 4: Slide 1 is a title slide. To add an image as the "fill" of the WordArt, go to **Insert**, **Picture**, and **WordArt**. Select WordArt style and type text in all capital letters.

Step 5: **Right click** on the **WordArt**, select **Format WordArt**, **Colors and Lines** tab. **Down arrow** at **Color** to **Fill Effects**, **Picture** tab.

Step 6: Go to **Picture** tab, **Select Picture**. Find image saved in My Pictures file. Select **Insert**. Click **OK**, then **OK** again on next screen. Image will "fill" the WordArt. Great fun!

Step 7: Continue adding text, images, and explanations. Get creative and imaginative with this project.

Step 8: Go to **File**, **Print**. **Print what**? Choices include: **Slides**, **Handouts 2**, **3**, **4**, **6**, **and 9 slides** per page, **Notes Pages** and **Outline View**. Experiment to see which format works best for your project.

figure **3.24**   figure **3.25**

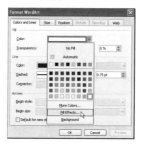

figure **3.26**

figure **3.27**

figure **3.28**

figure **3.29**

Information Literacy Standards for Student Learning

The student who is information literate accesses information efficiently and effectively.

The student who is information literate uses information accurately and creatively.

The student who is an independent learner is information literate and appreciates literature and other creative expressions of information.

NETS Standards:

• Students demonstrate a sound understanding of the nature and operation of technology systems.

Students use productivity tools to collaborate in constructing technology-enhanced models, prepare publications, and produce other creative works.

FLIP BOOKLET
Create a booklet that is new, different, and exciting!

Task Description: Students will research and report what they have learned in printed format. This is a hands-on, creative project, which will display student knowledge. The Flip Booklet encourages the use of varied technology skills plus cutting and pasting, in the old-fashioned sense of the words.

I. PLAN

Curricular Connections:

All topics, all grade levels, all degrees of difficulty.

Flip Booklets also a review technique.

Grade levels: 3-12

Subject Areas: All

Software: Word

II. PREPARE

❑ *Decide topics to be researched.*

❑ *Prepare a schedule for each student, if necessary, based on number of computers available.*

❑ *Practice changing margins in Word.*

❑ *Practice using columns in Word.*

❑ *Experiment with images, text boxes, and WordArt.*

III. PRESENT

Step 1: Explain research project to students. Display examples of flip booklets.

Step 2: Demonstrate techniques needed in Word and allow students time to research.

Step 3: Open **Word**, **File**, **New**, **Blank Document**.

Step 4: Go to **File**, **Page Setup**, **Margin** tab. Change **Margins** to:
Top 0.6 inches
Bottom 0.6 inches
Left 0 inches
Right 0 inches
Pop-up will appear advising that margins are set outside printable area. Click **Ignore**.

Step 5: **Format**, **Columns**, select **Two**. Select **Line Between**.

Step 6: Go to **View**, select **Ruler**. Draw lines to divide the page in thirds, approximately at 3 1/3 inches and 6 1/3 inches. This provides a visual guide for correct placement of text. Go to **View**, **Toolbars**, make sure that **Drawing** is selected. Click on the **Line** icon (a straight line) and draw the two lines needed.

Step 7: Page 1. Type three important words for the topic in the right hand column of the page. Use WordArt.

Step 8: Page 2. Same margins, same columns, same lines. Type information and add images in each column.

Step 9: Go to **File**, **Print**. Glue pages back to back, or print back to back. Fold lengthwise. Cut the "top" into thirds.

figure **3.30**

figure **3.31**

figure **3.32**

figure **3.33**

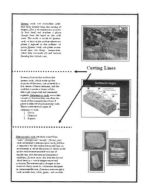

figure **3.34**

Information Literacy Standards for Student Learning

The student who is information literate uses information accurately and creatively.

The student who is an independent learner is information literate and appreciates literature and other creative expressions of information.

NETS Standards:

Students demonstrate a sound understanding of the nature and operation of technology systems.

Students are proficient in the use of technology.

Students use technology tools to enhance learning, increase productivity, and promote creativity.

HATS, CHAPEAUS, and SOMBREROS
Research is added to a hat shaped document … not as exciting as a sombrero or chapeau, but a hat none-the-less!

Task Description: Students will create a tri-cornered hat in PowerPoint, add researched information, and cut and fold the hat. This project is great bulletin board material. For variety, take the 8 1/2 x 11-inch paper and enlarge it on a copy machine to have different sized hats on display.

I. PLAN

Curricular Connections:

Research project for any topic.

Study of synonyms and antonyms.

Grade levels: 3-8

Subject Areas: All

Software: PowerPoint

II. PREPARE

❏ *Decide topics to be researched.*

❏ *Prepare a schedule for each student, if necessary, based on number of computers available.*

❏ *Experiment with PowerPoint. Use the ruler, change margins, line drawing, text boxes, and images.*

❏ *Practice making samples of hats. Find the best techniques to cut and fold.*

❏ *Prepare a display for the finished products. Make a banner for the display.*

III. PRESENT

Step 1: Introduce research project to students. Display samples of hat project.

Step 2: Demonstrate skills needed in PowerPoint. Allow students time to research topic.

Step 3: Open **PowerPoint**, **File**, **New**, **Blank Presentation**, **Blank Slide**.

Step 4: Go to **File**, **Page Setup**, change **Margins** to:
Width 11 inches
Height 8.5 inches

Step 5: Go to **View**, select **Ruler**. On Drawing Toolbar, select Auto Shapes, Lines. Draw two diagonal lines from the top center to 1 1/2 inches from the bottom right and left. Draw straight lines at 1/2 inch, 1 1/2 inches and 2 1/2 inches.

Step 6: Go to **Insert**, **Picture**, **ClipArt**. Find an appropriate image; insert it into the large triangle at the top. Change color to washout (watermark). **Right click** on **ClipArt**. Select **Format Picture**, **Picture** tab. **Down Arrow** at **Color**, select **Washout** and click **OK**.

Step 7: Go to **Insert**, **Text Box**. Add text and center it in the top triangle. Start with one word, then two, until the space is filled. Add images, ClipArt. Make it graphically fun and appealing.

Step 8: Go to **Insert**, **Picture**, **WordArt**, add the name of the person, place, or thing being researched in the one-inch space at the bottom.

Step 9: Go to **File**, **Print.** Fold hat and display!
Fold the two top corners to the back.
Make a crease on the 1 1/2-inch line. Fold up to the 2 1/2-inch line. Turn the 1/2-inch line back.
Glue or tape as needed.

figure **3.35**

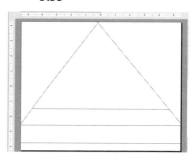

figure **3.36**

figure **3.37**

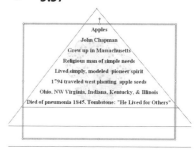

figure **3.38**

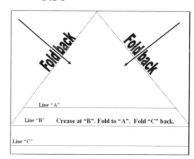

figure **3.39**

Information Literacy Standards for Student Learning

The student who is an independent learner is information literate and strives for excellence in information seeking and knowledge generation.

The student who is information literate uses information accurately and creatively.

NETS Standards:

Students use technology to locate, evaluate, and collect information from a variety of sources.

Students use technology tools to enhance learning, increase productivity, and promote creativity.

HERO HISTORY
Write the story of a favorite hero!

Task Description: Students will write a book, published as a mini book, about a hero. What makes a hero? This project allows students to examine the lives of famous or infamous people and decide if that person is truly a hero. The printed books are perfect for display or gifts to family members if a personal hero is chosen.

I. PLAN

Curricular Connections:

Research based project about a hero.

Project to honor a personal hero.

Grade levels: All

Subject Areas:

Language Arts

Library

History

Reading

Science

Technology

Software: PowerPoint

II. PREPARE

❏ *Decide topics for research.*

❏ *Prepare a schedule for each student, if necessary, based on number of computers available.*

❏ *Practice skills needed in PowerPoint. Review how to use text boxes, import images, different slide layouts.*

❏ *Review the printing options in PowerPoint.*

❏ *Create a list of databases for students to access.*

III. PRESENT

Step 1: Introduce the project. Display samples of hero history booklets.

Step 2: Demonstrate the skills needed to be successful in PowerPoint. Allow students time for research.

Step 3: Open **PowerPoint**, **File**, **New**, **Blank Presentation**. Slide layout of choice.

Step 4: **Insert**, **Picture**, **WordArt**. Add person's name in WordArt. Get creative! Hold cursor over icons on the Drawing Toolbar at the bottom of slide screen, and change the WordArt shape, style, shadow, or 3-D quality. Have fun experimenting with WordArt. Add a photograph of the person, if available.

Step 5: Go to **Format**, **Bullets and Numbering**, select any bullet. Add text in bulleted format. Writing must be concise. Please, do not use whole sentences, unless you are using a quotation.

Step 6: Change the bullets to represent the person. (Students must have an appropriate picture or ClipArt saved to My Pictures folder.) **Highlight bulleted text**. Go to **Format**, **Bullets and Numbering**, **Bulleted** tab. Click on **Picture**, **Import Picture**, find the picture, double click on it, and click **OK**.

Step 7: Continue adding text and images to complete the Hero History. Include a brief life history, a picture, a list of characteristics that makes the person special, and a quote from that person.

Step 8: Go to **File**, **Print**, **Handouts**, **2 per page**, **Frame Slides**. Cut apart, trim the edges, and staple together.

figure **3.40**

figure **3.41**

figure **3.42**

figure **3.43**

figure **3.44**

Information Literacy Standards for Student Learning

The student who is information literate uses information accurately and creatively.

The student who is an independent learner is information literate and strives for excellence in information seeking and knowledge generation.

NETS Standards:

Students use technology tools to locate, evaluate, and collect information from a variety of sources.

Students use technology tools to enhance learning, increase productivity, and promote creativity.

NONFICTION CONVENTIONS
Help students get a visual idea of the many nonfiction conventions!

Task Description: Students will create books, complete with a tour guide, to help learn about tables, labels, indexes, and all nonfiction conventions. Using a cartoon tour guide and comic book writing style will keep students interested.

I. PLAN

Curricular Connections:

Study of text structures.

Study of tables, labels, indexes, pictures, diagrams, maps, symbols, glossaries.

Display for the library or language arts class.

Grade levels: K-8

Subject Areas:

Language Arts

Library

Reading

Software: PowerPoint

II. PREPARE

❑ *Decide the order in which nonfiction conventions will be taught. This is not a one-day lesson.*

❑ *Prepare a schedule for each student, if necessary, based on number of computers available.*

❑ *Have books available to display conventions.*

❑ *Practice PowerPoint skills needed. Experiment with graphics, text boxes, images.*

❑ *Experiment with callouts on the drawing toolbar.*

❑ *Understand the options available in the print dialog box in PowerPoint.*

III. PRESENT

Step 1: Introduce topic to students. Show examples of the booklets.

Step 2: Demonstrate techniques used in PowerPoint, allow students time to search books and Web sites to find examples of each convention. Encourage them to be creative with their tour guide of the conventions. The tour guide can be made from ClipArt, something original that students created in Paint, or drew and scanned.

Step 3: Open **PowerPoint**, **File**, **New**, **Blank Presentation**, first a **Title Side** and thereafter use **Title**, **Text**, and **Content Layout**.

Step 4: First slide – title of project and introduction to the tour guide. To give voice to the tour guide, **Down Arrow** at **AutoShapes** on the **Drawing Toolbar**. Select **Callouts**.

Step 5: Adjust the callout exactly as you do ClipArt. Grab and pull one of the four corners to enlarge or decrease size. Rotate with the green circle at the top.

Step 6: Go to **Insert**, **Text Box** into the **Callout**. Add text to define and explain convention. Search for examples on the Internet.

Step 7: After each nonfiction convention lesson, have students add a slide to their on-going publication.

Step 8: When project is finished, go to **File**, **Print**, **Handouts**, **2 per page**, **Frame Slides**. Cut and staple or use paper fastener to make a book.

figure **3.45**

figure **3.46**

figure **3.47**

figure **3.48**

figure **3.49**

Information Literacy Standards for Student Learning

The student who is information literate evaluates information critically and competently.

The student who is an independent learner is information literate and appreciates literature and other creative expressions of information.

NETS Standards:

Students demonstrate a sound understanding of the nature and operation of technology systems.

Students are proficient in the use of technology.

Students use technology tools to enhance learning, increase productivity, and promote creativity.

POST CARDS
This fantastic project can be researched, created, and printed in one class session!

Task Description: Students will present research in a post card format. Each post card must have a picture or image representative of the topic, three to five facts about the topic in the message portion, and a stamp that is indicative of the topic. While making the post cards, many technology skills as well as researching skills are reinforced. Students enjoy creating post cards and their projects display beautifully.

I. PLAN

Curricular Connections:

Post cards can be created in any class for any topic.

Quick research idea. Each student is assigned a different aspect of a topic, researches it, makes a post card, and shares information.

Create post cards in heavier card stock with address on reverse side and send.

Grade levels: All

Subject Areas: All

Software: PowerPoint

II. PREPARE

❏ *Decide topic to be researched.*

❏ *Prepare a schedule for each student, if necessary, based on number of computers available.*

❏ *Practice skills needed in PowerPoint, adding images and text boxes, working with graphics.*

❏ *Experiment with drawing lines.*

❏ *Find acceptable sites for students to get pictures and images. Practice copy and paste techniques. www.pics4learning.com offers copyright free images. Plan a discussion of copyright rules and regulations.*

III. PRESENT

Step 1: Introduce post card project. Assign topics to students and display examples.

Step 2: Demonstrate PowerPoint techniques and allow students research time.

Step 3: Open **PowerPoint**, **File**, **New**, **Blank Presentation**, **Blank Slide**.

Step 4: Slide 1 is the picture side of the post card. Go to Web sites such as www. Pics4learning.com and find a picture. **Right Click** on that **image**, select **Copy** (left click). Return to PowerPoint, **Right Click** on slide; select **Paste** (left click). Resize image as needed by pulling on one of the four corners to change size proportionately.

Step 5: Slide 2, also **Blank Slide** layout, is the message, address, and stamp side of the post card. Go to **Insert**, **Text Box**. Add the message on the left hand side of the post card making certain that it includes 3-5 facts written about the topic.

Step 6: Go to **AutoShapes**, **Line** (or to Line icon on Drawing Toolbar). Draw a partial line down the middle of slide 2 and four lines for address on the right side of the post card.

Step 7: Go to **Insert**, **Picture**, **ClipArt**. Find an image representative of the topic. Insert it into the upper right hand corner of the post card. Resize and position as needed.

Step 8: Go to **File**, **Print**, **Handouts**, **2 per page**, **Frame Slides**. Cut two pieces and glue back to back.

figure **3.50**

figure **3.51**

figure **3.52**

figure **3.53**

figure **3.54**

QUILT IT
Get students busy designing a quilt!

Task Description: Student will display researched information by creating a single block of a quilt project and collaborating with their peers to assemble and finish the quilt. Display the students' work on bulletin boards. If you have time and a large budget, print students' quilt squares on transfer paper. Press the transfer onto muslin and make a fabric quilt that is sewn not glued.

I. PLAN

Curricular Connections:

Research about any topic, report findings in the form of a quilt square to be printed.

Art project about designs of different countries.

Math project to visualize area, perimeter, as well as researching mathematicians' lives and contributions.

Grade levels: All

Subject Areas:

Elective Areas

Language Arts

Library

Mathematics

Science

Social Studies

Software: PowerPoint

II. PREPARE

❏ *Decide topics to be researched.*

❏ *Prepare a schedule for each student, if necessary, based on number of computers available.*

❏ *Practice setting margins in PowerPoint.*

❏ *Practice finding and using graphics, text boxes in PowerPoint.*

❏ *Experiment with printing formats to decide which size the quilt blocks will be.*

III. PRESENT

Step 1: Discuss and introduce Quilt it project. Encourage creativity in students. Display examples.

Step 2: Demonstrate the skills needed in PowerPoint. Allow students time to research topics and collaborate with peers.

Step 3: In **PowerPoint**, **File**, **New**, **Blank Presentation**, **Slide Layout** of choice.

Step 4: Go to **File**, **Page Setup**. Change **Margin** width to **7.5 inches**.

Step 5: Go to **Insert**, **Picture**, **ClipArt**. Search for **Borders**. Suggestion: have all squares in the quilt use the same border to unify the project.

Step 6: Go to **Insert**, **Picture**, **WordArt**. Add title of quilt block in WordArt format. Creativity counts!

Step 7: Go to **Insert**, **Text Box**, add bullets of information. No sentences, please, just short, concise phrases.

Step 8: Go to **Insert**, **Picture**, **ClipArt** or **File**. Add images, ClipArt, photographs. Visually explain the topic.

Step 9: Go to **File**, **Print**, select the printing option of choice. The full slide will print at 7.5 x 7.5 inches, while handouts vary in size, from 3 x 3 inches for 4 handouts per page, 3 3/4 x 3 3/4 inches for 2 handouts per page and 2 1/4 x 2 1/4 inches for 6 handouts per page. Cut out individual quilt squares and join together decorating as much as possible.

figure **3.55**

figure **3.56**

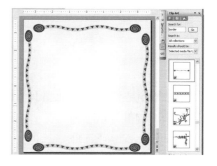

figure **3.57**

figure **3.58**

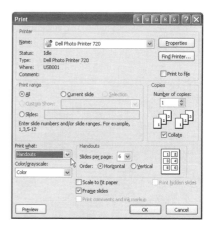

figure **3.59**

Information Literacy Standards for Student Learning

The student who is information literate evaluates information critically and competently.

The student who is information literate uses information accurately and creatively.

NETS Standards:

Students are proficient in the use of technology.

Students develop positive attitudes toward technology uses that support lifelong learning, collaboration, personal pursuits, and productivity.

Students use technology tools to enhance learning, increase productivity, and promote creativity.

TABLE TENTS
Do you need a way to display information? This is it!

> **Task Description:** Students will create table tents to display researched information. The table tent will exhibit the student's knowledge of a topic. This project is advertising and marketing at its best.

I. PLAN

Curricular Connections:

Genre displays: students define historical fiction, science fiction, fantasy, realistic fiction, poetry, folk tales, fairy tales, and biographies.

Text types: students define narrative, expository, technical, and persuasive text.

Science: rocks and minerals, chemicals, compounds.

Famous people - mini biography reporting.

Social Studies descriptions of events, maps.

Name tags for projects on display.

Creative advertising.

Beginning of school year or semester, student names for seating arrangements.

Grade levels: 3-12

Subject Areas: All

Software: PowerPoint

II. PREPARE

❑ *Decide topics to be researched or advertised.*

❑ *Prepare a schedule for each student, if necessary, based on number of computers available.*

❑ *Practice changing page setup in PowerPoint.*

❑ *Experiment with rotating text and graphics in PowerPoint.*

III. PRESENT

Step 1: Introduce concept of advertising information with a table tent. Stress the need for creativity and display examples of table tents.

Step 2: Demonstrate skills required in PowerPoint. Allow students time to gather researched information.

Step 3: Open **PowerPoint**, **File**, **New**, **Blank Presentation**, **Blank Slide**.

Step 4: Go to **File**, **Page Setup**. Change **Slides Sized for** to **Letter Paper, 8.5 x 11 inches**, change **Orientation** to **Portrait**.

Step 5: Go to **View**. Select **Ruler**.

Step 6: Go to **Insert**, **Text Box**. Add information and "drag" it to the bottom one-half of the page leaving a 1 1/2-inch space at the bottom.

Step 7: Go to **Insert**, **Picture**, **WordArt**. Add title and "drag" it to the top one-half of the page, again leaving a 1 1/2-inch space but this time at the top of the page. Select the WordArt and experiment with all of the different editing tools on the **Drawing Toolbar**. Hold the cursor over each icon to see changes can be made. Experiment with changing the Shadow Style, 3D Style, Line Style, Format, WordArt Shape, WordArt Same Letter Height, WordArt Vertical Text, WordArt Alignment, or WordArt Character Spacing. Students love this part of any design work.

Step 8: Next **Rotate WordArt**. **Grab** the green handle and swing the WordArt so it is upside down.

Step 9: Go to **File**, **Print**. Fold in half horizontally and crease well. Fold top and bottom margins in and crease. Glue, tape, or staple bottom of tent (top and bottom margins).

figure **3.60**

figure **3.61**

figure **3.62**

figure **3.63**

figure **3.64**

Information Literacy Standards for Student Learning

The student who is information literate uses information accurately and creatively.

The student who contributes positively to the learning community and to society is information literate and recognizes the importance of information to a democratic society.

NETS Standards:

Students demonstrate a sound understanding of the nature and operation of technology systems.

Students use technology tools to process data and report results.

Students use technology tools to enhance learning, increase productivity, and promote creativity.

TOTEM POLES
Students will research the history of totem poles, choose five symbols to represent their families, and create a family totem pole!

Task Description: Student will learn how families in the Pacific Northwest carved totem poles that were displayed at the home's front entrance symbolizing the qualities, experiences, and exploits of the family. To create totem poles was and is a very creative process. This project encourages student to think about his or her own families, and extend those thoughts to other cultures, other families. How have we all changed? How have we stayed the same?

I. PLAN

Curricular Connections:

Research of different cultures.

History of Native Americans.

Art study of carvings.

Language Arts study of symbolism.

Grade levels: All

Subject Areas:

Art

Language Arts

Library

Reading

Social Studies

Software: PowerPoint

II. PREPARE

❏ *Decide topics to be researched. What aspect of totem poles are students learning?*

❏ *Prepare a schedule for each student, if necessary, based on number of computers available.*

❏ *Practice changing page setup in PowerPoint.*

❏ *Practice importing graphics, ClipArt, working with text boxes.*

III. PRESENT

Step 1:   Introduce topic of totem poles. Discuss how creative Native Americans were in their carvings and representations of their lives. Show samples.

Step 2:   Demonstrate skills needed in PowerPoint. Allow students time to gather information and research family traits.

Step 3:   Open **PowerPoint**, **File**, **New**, **Blank Presentation**, **Blank Slide**.

Step 4:   Go to **File**, **Page Setup**. Change **Margins** to:
Width 7.5 inches
Height 10 inches
Orientation of slides Portrait

Step 5:   On the **Drawing Toolbar**, **Down Arrow** at **AutoShapes**, select **Trapezoid**. Draw a tall totem pole shape. Make the shape fill the slide.

Step 6:   Find a graphic of tree bark. Save it in My Pictures folder. To fill totem pole with bark, **Right Click** on shape. Select **Format Auto Shapes**. On Format AutoShape screen, **Down Arrow** at **Color** and select **Fill Effects**, **Texture Tab**, select **Other Texture**; find the bark texture in My Pictures folder. Click **OK** and **OK** again. Bark will fill the tree trunk.

Step 7:   Go to **Insert**, **Picture**, **ClipArt**. Find images to represent the family. Stack the images on the totem pole.

Step 8:   Go to **File**, **Print**. Students will present the story of their family totems to the class.

figure **3.65**

figure **3.66**

figure **3.67**

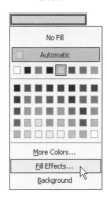

figure **3.68**

figure **3.69**

Information Literacy Standards for Student Learning

The student who is information literate accesses information efficiently and effectively.

The student who is information literate uses information accurately and creatively.

NETS Standards:

Students are proficient in the use of technology.

Students demonstrate a sound understanding of the nature and operation of technology systems.

Students use technology tools to enhance learning, increase productivity, and promote creativity.

TRI-FOLD BROCHURES
Create a research-based brochure.
This project uses many technology tools and skills!

Task Description: Students will research information, organize, and share it in a tri-fold brochure format. This project can be created using Microsoft's Publisher software. However, not everyone has Publisher. The skills learned by preparing a brochure in Word are many, varied, and good to know.

I. PLAN

Curricular Connections:

Brochures for information about any subject.

Brochures to advertise event.

Library brochures for at home use of databases, information about library hours.

Grade levels: 5-12

Subject Areas: All

Software: Word

II. PREPARE

❑ *Decide topics to be researched, advertised.*

❑ *Prepare a schedule for each student, if necessary, based on number of computers available.*

❑ *Practice changing margins in Word.*

❑ *Practice inserting columns and page breaks in Word.*

❑ *Practice inserting ClipArt and images.*

❑ *Experiment with formatting text boxes.*

❑ *Make diagram for students of column placement on two pages.*

III. PRESENT

Step 1: Explain project to students. Show examples of professionally made brochures and samples other students have made. Give students the diagram of column placement.

Step 2: Demonstrate skills needed in Word. Allow students time to research.

Step 3: Open **Word**, **File**, **New**, **Blank Document**.

Step 4: Go to **File**, **Page Setup**, **Margins**. Change to **0.3** inches all around and click **Ignore** when pop-up box says that the margins are too small. Change **Orientation** to **Landscape**.

Step 5: Go to **Format**, **Columns**, and select **Three**. Change the **Spacing** between the columns to 0.6 inches (double whatever the margins are). Click **OK**.

Step 6: Click **Show/Hide** ¶ on the **Standard** toolbar. This enables you to see the formatting that will be applied to the document. The editing marks do not print. Put the cursor at the top of the first column, go to **Insert**, **Break**, and **Column Break**, and click **OK**. Do the same at the top of the second column. The text will now automatically wrap to the top of the next column.

Step 7: Do a **File**, **Save As** and name this file **Brochure Page 2**. Next, begin working on the page and save it as **Brochure Page 1**. Working this as two separate pages is much easier.

Step 8: Add text, WordArt, ClipArt, images to the brochure. **Select** one of the **images**, **right click**, and select **Format Text Box**. Choose **Layout** tab, **Tight**. Text will wrap around image.

Step 9: Go to **File**, **Print**. Print two pages, glue back to back, and fold in thirds.

figure **3.70**

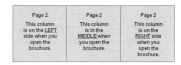

figure **3.71**

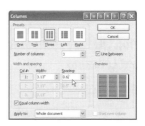

figure **3.72**

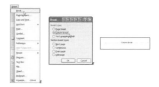

figure **3.73**

figure **3.74**

figure **3.75**

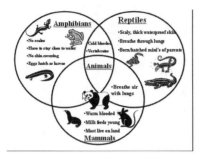

Information Literacy Standards for Student Learning

The student who is information literate evaluates information critically and competently.

The student who is an independent learner is information literate and strives for excellence in information seeking and knowledge generation.

NETS Standards:

Students demonstrate a sound understanding of the nature and operation of technology systems.

Students use technology to locate, evaluate, and collect information from a variety of sources.

Students are proficient in the use of technology.

VENN DIAGRAMS
Compare and contrast anything and everything!

Task Description: Students will research topics and visually organize comparisons and contrasts between ideas, objects, and topics. Excellent thinking skills are used when working on Venn Diagrams. Younger students can work with two circles, older students with three. This project will provide an amazing bulletin board display. Venn diagrams are not just for mathematics anymore. Think of the possibilities.

I. PLAN

Curricular Connections:

Language Arts - compare and contrast stories, poems, themes, genres, characters.

Mathematics - compare and contrast shapes, sets, rules.

Physical Education - compare and contrast games, rules, equipment.

Science - compare and contrast theories, laws, scientists, and their contributions.

Social Studies - compare and contrast people, places, and events.

Grade levels: All

Subject Areas: All

Software: PowerPoint

II. PREPARE

❑ *Decide topics to be researched.*

❑ *Prepare a schedule for each student, if necessary, based on number of computers available.*

❑ *Practice drawing equal circles in PowerPoint.*

❑ *Practice adding text boxes, images, ClipArt.*

❑ *Prepare a worksheet for students so that they can write the comparisons and contrasts first.*

III. PRESENT

Step 1: Introduce Venn diagrams and the different ways they can be used. Show examples.

Step 2: Demonstrate the techniques needed in PowerPoint for the completion of a successful project. Allow students time to research and complete the compare, and contrast document.

Step 3: Open **PowerPoint**, **File**, **New**, **Blank Presentation**, **Blank Slide.**

Step 4: Select **Oval icon** on **Drawing Toolbar**. Hold **CTRL** key and **draw** a circle. When correct size, **select** (click on) the shape, go to **Edit**, **Duplicate**. This will insure that each circle is exactly the same size. Draw two or three circles depending upon the project requirements.

Step 5: Select each of the circles, click on **Fill Color icon** (paint can) on **Drawing Toolbar** and change to **No Fill**.

Step 6: Go to **Insert**, **Text Box**. Fill each circle with researched information. Put shared information in the intersection of the circles. No whole sentences please! There is not enough room. Bullets of information are the best to use.

Step 7: Go to **Insert**, **Picture**, then to ClipArt, images From File, WordArt. Add interest to the Venn diagrams.

Step 8: Go to **File**, **Print**.

figure **3.76**

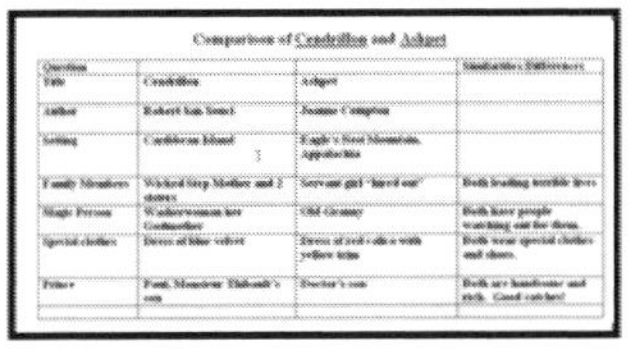

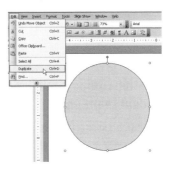

figure **3.77**

figure **3.78**

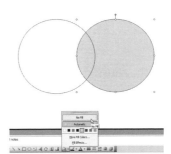

figure **3.79**

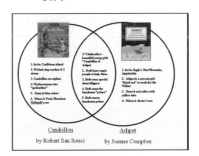

figure **3.80**

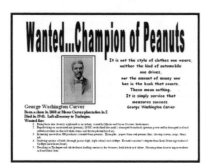

Information Literacy Standards for Student Learning

The student who is information literate uses information accurately and creatively.

The student who is an independent learner is information literate and appreciates literature and other creative expressions of information.

NETS Standards:

Students are proficient in the use of technology.

Students use technology tools to enhance learning, increase productivity, and promote creativity.

Students use technology to locate, evaluate, and collect information from a variety of sources.

WANTED POSTER
Chronicle the famous and the infamous in history!

Task Description: Students will create informative "Wanted Posters," imitating the posters of old. Researched information adds credibility and accuracy to the poster. Students will enjoy manipulating the layout of the information, images, and ClipArt. These posters make a phenomenal bulletin board. It is incredible how creative students become with this assignment.

I. PLAN

Curricular Connections:

Autobiographical, the student is wanted from something.

Bacteria need to be eradicated.

Diseases, stamp out diseases.

Inventors, who were they and what did they do?

Famous historical figures, this is a fun one!

Literary figures - poets, authors, playwrights.

Pollution, how can we get rid of it?

Scientists, so many from which to choose.

Sports' Stars, many of these people too.

Grade levels: 3-12
Subject Areas: All
Software: Word

II. PREPARE

- ❑ *Decide topic of research.*
- ❑ *Prepare a worksheet that has listing of all information required. Create a rubric for students' use.*
- ❑ *Prepare a schedule for each student, if necessary, based on number of computers available.*
- ❑ *Experiment with images, formatting text boxes, text-wrapping features in Word.*
- ❑ *Practice inserting text boxes, images, ClipArt, WordArt in Word.*
- ❑ *Find databases for students to use for research.*
- ❑ *Provide students with a list of police jargon, which is fun to use on Wanted Posters.*

III. PRESENT

Step 1: Discuss posters of the Old West, the "Wanted, Dead, or Alive" formats. Show samples of the Wild West versions, as well as the FBI's 10 Most Wanted Fugitives posters, available on the FBI Web sites.

Step 2: Demonstrate skills and techniques needed in Word. Provide time to research the person, place, or events going on a wanted poster.

Step 3: Open **Word**, **File**, **New**, **Blank Document**.

Step 4: Go to **File**, **Page Setup**. Change **Margins** to **0.5 inches** all around. Students select **Portrait** or **Landscape** Orientation. Students can choose.

Step 5: Go to **Insert**, **Picture**, **WordArt**. Add title. Click **OK**.

Step 6: A suggestion is to fill WordArt with an image representative of the topic. Have an image saved in My Pictures folder. Use all capital letters for WordArt. **Right Click** on **WordArt**, select **Format WordArt**, **Colors and Lines** tab, **Down Arrow** at **Color** to **Fill Effects**, **Picture tab**, **Select Picture**. Find picture in My Pictures file, click **Insert**. Then **OK** and **OK** on next two screens. Image will be the background of the WordArt. This procedure takes many steps, but the results are well worth it.

Step 7: Go to **Insert**, **Text Box**. Add information with no sentences, just bullets of information. Select the text, **Format**, **Bullets and Numbering**, **Bulleted** tab. Select bullet and click **OK**.

Step 8: Go to **Insert, Picture, From File**. Find a saved picture and insert it. **Right Click** on the text box, select **Format Text Box**, **Layout** tab, **Tight**.

Step 9: Go to **File**, **Print**.

figure **3.81**

figure **3.82**

figure **3.83**

figure **3.84**

figure **3.85**

Information Literacy Standards for Student Learning

The student who is information literate accesses information efficiently and effectively.

The student who is information literate uses information accurately and creatively.

The student who is an independent learner is information literate and appreciates literature and other creative expressions of information.

NETS Standards:

Students demonstrate a sound understanding of the nature and operation of technology systems.

Students use technology tools to enhance learning, increase productivity, and promote creativity.

Students use technology to locate, evaluate, and collect information from a variety of sources.

WHEN DID THAT HAPPEN?
Timelines are a visual representation of information. Excel makes easy work of a timeline!

Task Description: Students will create timelines about any topic. Timelines inspire quality research, excellent technology skills, and are great projects to display.

I. PLAN

Curricular Connections:

Art, any period in art can be researched.

Music, musicians, types of music.

Science, discoveries, events, inventors.

English, literature trends, character developments.

Food and Consumer Science, history of food groups, restaurants, cooking techniques.

Inventions, who invented what, when and where?

Cultures, how did the cultures develop and when?

Agriculture, which came first the chicken or the egg?

History - people, places, events.

Family Journal and biographical information.

Explorers, when and where did these brave ancestors travel?

Transportation, this is huge, from walking to horses to the space exploration.

And more …

Grade levels: 4-12

Subject Areas: All

Software: Excel

II. PREPARE

❑ *Decide topics to be researched.*

❑ *Prepare a schedule for each student, if necessary, based on number of computers available.*

❑ *Practice adding information to cells in Excel. Experiment with formatting of text.*

❑ *Learn how to place borders around cells in Excel.*

❑ *Experiment with addition of graphics to the timeline.*

❑ *Prepare a worksheet for students to sketch timeline on paper before entering information into Excel.*

III. PRESENT

Step 1: Introduce timeline project. Show samples of timelines.

Step 2: Demonstrate skills needed in Excel. Allow time for research. Students record timeline information on worksheet first.

Step 3: Open **Excel**, **File**, **New**, **Blank Workbook**.

Step 4: Go to **File**, **Page Setup**, **Margins**. **Change** to **0.5 inches** all around. Change **Orientation** to **Landscape**.

Step 5: Go to **Insert**, **Picture**, **WordArt**. Add title. Spread across the worksheet.

Step 6: Skip several lines and begin adding text to cells. **Add text** for each date in the cell above or below, whichever looks best. Format the text. **Select cells**, click on **Format**, **Cells**, **Alignment** tab. **Check** the box next to **Wrap Text.** Determine **Orientation** of text by clicking and dragging red diamond to the desired degree. Click **OK**.

Step 7: Adjust row height if needed by placing mouse on line between row numbers. When mouse turns to cross hair, click and drag up or down. Adjust the column width with the same technique. Place cursor on the line between the column headings and click and drag.

Step 8: Place borders around cells of timeline. Go to **View**, **Toolbars**, and select **Borders**. Highlight cells. Click **Down Arrow** on **Borders** toolbar and select option.

Step 9: Go to **Insert**, **Picture**, **ClipArt**. Adding pictures and ClipArt will enhance timeline.

Step 10: Go to **File**, **Print**. If the timeline prints as more than one page, cut and tape it together.

figure **3.86**

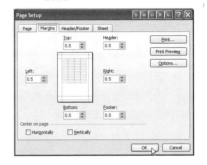

figure **3.87**

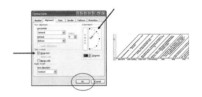

figure **3.88**

figure **3.89**

Conclusion

So, there you have fifty projects to try with your students. Please experiment and have fun with these ideas. Encourage your students to read, research, and present what they have learned in new, different, and exciting ways. You will not only challenge yourself and your students but you will also add new dimensions to your teaching skills.

Be sure to **plan**, **prepare**, and **present** the lessons that appeal to you and work with your individual curricula and standards. Hands-on learning is without a doubt the most rewarding for students. The projects that they make today will be remembered for many years to come. Remember the pâpier-mâché fruits and vegetables, the sugar cube igloo stuck together with white paste, and Homer Price's donuts made of cheerios? Those creations were made more years ago than I care to admit … and are still among the memories I carry with me. Give your students the same opportunities to show what they know with projects of all shapes and sizes.

Evaluate student work with rubrics that you have prepared with the help of Web sites devoted to make your lives easier or that your gifted students have prepared as a differentiated component of the assignment. Self-evaluation is appropriate and oftentimes quite informative. Students can also work on peer-evaluations. You know your students well and can decide what is appropriate.

The projects in this book were written specifically for Microsoft software. If you work with a Macintosh product, please read the directions and experiment with the toolbars and icons that are available in the programs that you have. They have to be somewhat similar. If all else fails, the Help menu, or your students, should be able to assist you.

Above all, please enjoy the activities and time spent with your students as you read, write, learn together, and produce more projects than you ever thought possible!